The Andrew R. Cecil Lectures on Moral Values in a Free Society

established by

The University of Texas at Dallas

Volume XV

Previous Volumes of the Andrew R. Cecil Lectures
on Moral Values in a Free Society

INDIVIDUALISM AND SOCIAL
RESPONSIBILITY

Individualism and Social Responsibility

ANDREW R. CECIL
HARVEY C. MANSFIELD
GEORGE WEIGEL
RICHARD S. LOMBARD
JAMES A. JOSEPH
JEAN BETHKE ELSHTAIN
JAROSLAV PELIKAN

With an Introduction by
ANDREW R. CECIL

Edited by
W. LAWSON TAITTE

The University of Texas at Dallas
1994

Library of Congress Catalog Card Number 94-60300
International Standard Book Number 0-292-71175-1

Distributed by the University of Texas Press,
Box 7819, Austin, Texas 78712

FOREWORD

The University of Texas at Dallas established the Andrew R. Cecil Lectures on Moral Values in a Free Society in 1979 to provide an opportunity for examining important issues that face our society. Each year since, U.T. Dallas has invited to its campus scholars, businessmen and members of the professions, public officials, and other notable individuals to share their ideas on these issues with the academic community and the general public. Over the fifteen years of their existence, the Cecil Lectures have become a valued tradition for the University and for the wider community. Distinguished authorities in many fields have participated in the program; their lectures have enriched the experience of all those who heard them or read the published proceedings of each series. They have enlarged our understanding of the system of moral values on which our country was founded and continues to rest.

The University named this program for Dr. Andrew R. Cecil, its Distinguished Scholar in Residence. During his tenure as President of The Southwestern Legal Foundation, Dr. Cecil's innovative leadership brought that institution into the forefront of continuing legal education in the United States. When he retired from the Foundation as its Chancellor Emeritus, Dr. Cecil was asked by U.T. Dallas to serve as its Distinguished Scholar in Residence, and the Cecil Lectures were instituted. In 1990, the Board of Regents of The University of Texas System established the Andrew R. Cecil Chair of Applied Ethics. It is appropriate that the Lectures and the Chair honor a man who has been concerned throughout his career with the moral foundations of our society and who has stressed his belief in the dignity and worth of every individual.

The fifteenth annual series of the Cecil Lectures, held on the University's campus on November 8 through 11, 1993, examined the theme of "Individualism and Social Responsibility." On behalf of U.T. Dallas, I would like to express our gratitude to Prof. Harvey C. Mansfield, Mr. George Weigel, Mr. Richard S. Lombard, Mr. James A. Joseph, Prof. Jean Bethke Elshtain, Prof. Jaroslav Pelikan, and Dr. Cecil for their willingness to share their ideas and for the outstanding lectures that are preserved in this volume of proceedings.

I also wish to express on behalf of the University our sincere thanks to all those who have helped make this program an important part of the life of the University, especially the contributors to the Lectures. Through their support these donors enable us to continue this important program and to publish the proceedings of the series, thus assuring a wide and permanent audience for the ideas the books contain.

I am confident that everyone who reads *Individualism and Social Responsibility*, the Andrew R. Cecil Lectures on Moral Values in a Free Society Volume XV, will be stimulated by the ideas presented in its seven essays.

ROBERT H. RUTFORD, President
The University of Texas at Dallas
March 1994

CONTENTS

INTRODUCTION

by

Andrew R. Cecil

In May 1891, Pope Leo XIII issued the famous and far-reaching encyclical *Rerum Novarum* ("New Things"). Addressed primarily to European countries, it raised a powerful voice of opposition against the shameful treatment of men "like chattels to make money by" and against "the wretchedness pressing so heavily and unjustly at this moment on the vast majority of the working classes." The encyclical emphasized that "labor is not a commodity" and sought remedies against the very rich, who "have been able to lay upon the teeming masses of the laboring poor a yoke little better than that of slavery itself."

Among the suggested remedies were legislation to "protect women and children from oppressive employment" and help from the state for wage earners, "who are undoubtedly among the weak and necessitous" and, therefore, "should be specially cared for and protected by the commonwealth." Thus, the Pope challenged the philosophy of laissez-faire, which advocated for the state the role of a "passive policeman" with functions limited to the preservation of public order and protection of private property.

One hundred years after the *Rerum Novarum* encyclical, Pope John Paul II released his encyclical *Centesimus Annus* ("The Hundredth Year") in which he endorses a "free economy" provided that it meets important challenges. The Pope asks, "Can it perhaps be said that, after

11

the failure of Communism, capitalism is the victorious social system, and that capitalism should be the goal of the countries now making efforts to rebuild their economy and society?"

The answer is: "If by capitalism is meant an economic system which recognizes the fundamental and positive role of business, the market, private property, and the resulting responsibility for the means of production, as well as free human creativity in the economic sector, then the answer is certainly in the affirmative." The reply is negative if by capitalism is meant a "ruthless" system based on self-interest with no moral concern for our fellowman, a system criticized by Pope Leo XIII a century ago.

Society is a product of man's social nature. A human being is a being of infinite worth, and his needs are the ultimate foundation of all government. It is the responsibility of the individuals that form society, as well as of society as a whole, to secure freedom and equal opportunity for all—the strong and the weak, the talented and the handicapped. Persons are not to be regarded as economic expendables or commodities; we have a sacred obligation to make every effort to enable others to live in decency.

In the second half of this century, we have seen an enormous expansion in the field of individual and human rights. In promoting maximum opportunity for the development of the individual, however, we should avoid the danger of an overgrown individualism striving only for personal gain, leading toward injustice and exploitation.

Individualism implies freedom of choice and equality of opportunity. This does not mean that it should be limited to the pursuit of private interest. It must pass the test of constructive service to the entire society. An individual may pursue his own good in his own way, but only so long as he does not attempt to deprive others of their freedom or impede their efforts to obtain it.

In determining the needs to be satisfied by society, moral and spiritual values cannot be ignored or forgotten. They are a trust and a challenge to inspire our conscience to seek a moral order in every relationship, including the social order. A major part of such concerns throughout the centuries has been caring for the unfortunate. This has been a constant theme of our Judeo-Christian heritage.

As far back as the fourth century, St. Ambrose preached: "Thou then, who has received the gift of God, thinkest thou that thou committed no injustice by keeping to thyself alone what would be the means of life to many? It is the bread of the hungry that thou keepest, it is the clothing of the naked that thou lockest up; the money that thou buried is the redemption of the wretched."

In our own century, the Swiss theologian Karl Barth (1886–1968) wrote: "The Church is witness to the fact that the Son of Man came to seek and to save the lost. And this implies—casting all false impartiality aside—the Church must concentrate first on the lower and lowest levels of society. The poor, the socially and economically weak and threatened, will always be the object of its primary and particular concern, and it will always insist on the State's special responsibility for these weaker members of society." (*Community, Church and State*, Peter Smith Press, 1960, p. 173.)

That responsibility does not stop at seeing that the poor are clothed and fed. A society's conscience cannot be at complete ease until all its members are integrated into it by means of responsible livelihood and active participation in its life.

In my lecture, "Individualism and Social Conscience," I stress the importance of social conscience in creating conditions that secure freedom and equal opportunity for all. The free world has demonstrated convincingly that the best system for providing conditions that will result in a high degree of prosperity is the one in which governmental interference and restrictions upon the freedom of the individual are limited. However, the maintenance of a system of private property, free initiative, and competition does not imply a policy of leaving things as they are. Overgrown individualism striving only for personal gain can result in injustice and exploitation. The history of the Industrial Revolution gives a vivid picture of this danger.

Social conscience vests in the government the responsibility to preserve the lives of the members of our communities and to protect them against physical violence, as well as against natural agents that threaten their health, such as floods, epidemics, and crippling diseases. When faced with unemployment, the proliferation of slums, and the deterioration of our cities and of the natural environment, social conscience calls for some form of governmental intervention. Through our government we plan for the conservation of natural resources, limit monopolies, and foster public education, in spite of the fact that at the time these programs were introduced they were proclaimed to be socialistic endeavors.

Society is a product of man's social nature. His needs are the ultimate foundation of all government; his interest in creating a system of government authority is to keep it in the service of humanity and to prevent it from being turned against him. The responsibilities that we have vested in government make social man a political man.

In his lecture "Responsibility and Its Perversions," Professor Harvey C. Mansfield examines the history of the idea of responsibility in a political context. He shows that it is a virtue of life in a republic, as opposed to the older aristocratic virtues, such as magnanimity or wit. A government based on rights and interests requires individual responsibility, and responsibility requires that an individual exercise initiative to accomplish what must be done. In Professor Mansfield's view, many of the current controversies that plague our political life result from misinterpretations of the idea of responsibility. These misinterpretations include passivity, selflessness, and self-expression.

Religious and spiritual values are interconnected with our political life and our social obligations. "There is an unbroken history," according to a relatively recent Supreme Court decision, "of official acknowledgement by all three branches of government of the role of religion in American life from at least 1789." The concept of a "wall" of separation between church and state is, therefore, "a useful figure of speech" but "is not a wholly accurate description of the practical aspects of the relationship that in fact exists." (*Lynch v. Donnelly*, 104 S. Ct. 1355, 1359 [1984].)

The metaphor of a "wall" (derived from Thomas Jefferson's reply to an address by a committee of the Danbury Baptist Association, January 1, 1802) serves as a reminder that the object of the First Amendment was to

prevent the formation of any national ecclesiastical
establishment that had the exclusive patronage of the
national government. But the fact remains that we do
not live in a vacuum, and an attempt to enforce a regime
of total separation of church and state, a separation
never intended by the First Amendment and uniformly
rejected by the Supreme Court, will only undermine our
national traditions, our religious heritage, and the ultimate constitutional objective of the First Amendment.

Under no circumstances should moral considerations
be eliminated in assessing our political goals. Christianity has influenced, more or less, all our institutions, customs, and relations, as well as our individual modes of
thinking and acting. Without the general direction of a
moral code, human society becomes aimless and meaningless; still the church should not try to control the government or to become an instrument of the state.

In sovereign reverence for the intentions of the framers
of our Constitution, we should not expect the state to behave as if it were a church or the church to behave as if it
were a state. There is always the peril of brutalizing the
City of God by associating it with the game of politics in
the City of Man. The City of God loses its spiritual purity
when it associates itself with man-made dogmas and the
means used in the City of Man to succeed in practical
politics.

Mr. George Weigel in his lecture "Building the Culture
of Freedom: Catholic Social Thought and the American
Experiment" examines the relationship between church
and state in detail. In discussing the encyclical *Centesimus Annus* that was mentioned above, he points out that
Pope John Paul II begins with the concept of human
freedom and suggests that the pope's message should be

of interest even to citizens who are not members of the Catholic church. Like that of Leo XIII a century before, John Paul II bases his teaching on the premise that the dignity and worth of each individual human being is a result of being created "in the image and likeness of God."

Mr. Weigel gives much of the credit for the liberation of Eastern Europe from the tyranny of totalitarianism to the pope's inspiration. According to the pope's teaching, the very nature of man requires a disciplined freedom. The totalitarian countries failed because they lacked that freedom. There is a warning to us insofar as we lack the discipline and wisdom to use our freedom wisely. The ideas in *Centesimus Annus* promise to transform Catholic social teaching in many areas, including the area of care for the poor and the oppressed.

From the Middle Ages down at least to the middle of the sixteenth century, the fundamental assumption about the relationship between economic realities and moral attitudes was that economic activity should be subordinated to traditional morality as it was expounded by the church. Although the church itself was a highly organized financial institution, the social teaching of the church looked at commerce as a dangerous activity and at trade as an occupation that serves, according to St. Thomas Aquinas, "the lust of gain."

Only at the end of the sixteenth century did signs of a divorce of economic realities from religious doctrines become evident. The divorce became final during the seventeenth and eighteenth centuries—an era of progress in economic thought, of growth in trade (described by a member of the British Parliament as the "fairest mistress in the world"), and of the recognition of economics as a subject for scientific study.

Private property was no longer regarded as a necessary evil but became one of the most important human rights, anterior to the existence of the state. Referring to this right, Locke argued that the "supreme power cannot take from any man any part of his property without his consent." The expansion of trade, the accumulation of wealth, and an irrepressible drive for economic gain were no longer denounced by saints and sages. Instead they became virtues that contributed to the conquest of the world.

Although economic efficiency is indispensable to the success of a businessman, such a success cannot endure when it is divorced from moral considerations and when the businessman's activities violate the rights of his fellowman to self-respect and dignity. In the long run, what is morally wrong can never be economically fruitful, and no economic action can be sound unless it fits into an accepted system of values. Expediency does not preclude the entrepreneur's concern for the welfare of his fellowman. It was Dr. Samuel Johnson who said that "a decent provision for the poor is a true test of civilization."

Accepting social responsibility is not only an ethical precept but is also the wisdom and law of life. In order to succeed economically, the businessman has to channel his efforts, talents, energies, and intelligence into avenues that will lead his business to prosper. His efforts, however, must be combined with his responsibility for promoting the well-being of the society in which he lives. Such responsibility does not undermine the springs of free initiative—the cornerstone of business endeavor in a free society.

In his lecture "Corporate Social Responsibilities in the Nineties," Mr. Richard S. Lombard points out two types of social responsibilities of corporations. The first kind of responsibility inheres in the nature of the corporation itself: It must use its resources and its people wisely in order to remain in being. Mr. Lombard contends that staying profitable and meeting the needs and expectations of shareholders and of the public are moral concerns for those to whom the reins of a business have been entrusted.

The other moral responsibilities of a corporation, according to Mr. Lombard, change with the evolving expectations of the public. Of course, officers and employees of a company must obey the laws that a society enacts. But they must also avoid offending the consensus of feeling about other issues that have not yet been formulated into law. Because of the rapid shifts in public attitudes—and because of differing expectations in the various countries in which multinational corporations do business—meeting the people's expectations has become increasingly complex over the years. In some countries, for instance, corporations are not expected or encouraged to make philanthropic contributions. In the United States, however, helping those in need has become an important part of corporate life.

Our nation has long recognized its responsibility to reach out to those in distress, not only in this country but also to those from other parts of the world. In his letter of December 2, 1783, to the "Volunteer Association and Other Inhabitants of the Kingdom of Ireland," General George Washington wrote:

"The bosom of America is open to receive not only the Opulent and respectable Strange, but the oppressed and persecuted of all Nations and Religions whom we shall welcome to a participation of all our rights and privileges, if by decency and propriety of conduct they appear to merit the enjoyment." (*The Writings of George Washington*, Vol. 27, ed. John C. Fitzpatrick, Greenwood Press, 1938, p. 254.)

A century and a half later, on April 28, 1938, President Franklin D. Roosevelt remarked in an address to the Daughters of the American Revolution: "Remember, remember always, that all of us, and you and I especially, are descended from immigrants and revolutionists." The large number of ethnic minorities that this country has welcomed makes us a "nation of immigrants." For the more than two centuries of our history, it has been the American dream that this array of cultures and heritages should somehow blend into one new entity. The American dream has been to become the "melting pot" in which a multitude of ethnic and cultural identities are fused into a single nation.

This dream, however, has never been fully realized. Racism has always been, and still remains, inconsistent with equality of rights as they pertain to citizenship and with the personal liberty which ought to be enjoyed by everyone within this free land of ours. Discriminatory systems have affected not only social and political relations in this country but have also resulted in economic inequities.

The issue of the integration of minorities into the main stream of American life looms as one of the most important confronting our nation. Until recently most immigrants to the United States were of European origins; the principal exception was the black population largely brought to this country by force. At present the non-European elements in our society are the faster-growing components of the population. Ethnic groups that trace their origins to Africa, Latin America, and Asia will continue to play an even more important role in American culture and society. In facing the multiracial, multicultural society of the future, we must learn to accommodate a multiplicity of ethnic, linguistic, religious, and cultural elements.

In his lecture "Pluralism and Civil Society: The Changing Civic Culture," Mr. James A. Joseph reminds us that even as long ago as the early nineteenth century Alexis de Tocqueville understood that the United States had developed a number of nongovernmental institutions that bound its citizens together in a multiplicity of ties. Churches, social and fraternal organizations, charitable institutions, and many other frameworks enabled Americans to cooperate and build a better society.

As Mr. Joseph points out, such institutions only work in an atmosphere of mutual respect. Too often in our history, there has been a lack of respect given to those who were different in race, religion, or country of origin. In an era in which our nation is becoming increasingly diverse, this principle of mutual respect must be cultivated so that we solve our common problems together in an atmosphere of peace and tolerance.

Professor Jean Bethke Elshtain in her lecture "Multiculturalism and Political Responsibility" laments the loss of this mutual respect. Increasingly, in her view, we are becoming a fragmented society. Instead of speaking as individuals, many have adopted the stance of a particular group to the exclusion of all other groups. If this trend continues, our very identity as a nation could be threatened. We can only exercise political responsibility if we understand ourselves to be parts of one common body.

Professor Elshtain believes that part of the educational process for each student must be an education for citizenship. Finding a common national identity, however, does not mean that our differences must be discounted. The best strains of American thought have always understood that the variety of experiences that the people who compose our society can bring to bear on our common purpose is one of the great strengths of the American heritage.

The idea of education for citizenship has been recognized since the earliest days of our country. Jefferson recommended for the "ordinary" man a curriculum of chiefly historical studies, while for the intellectual elite he prescribed classical and scientific studies. The wide horizon of Jefferson's vision put him in advance of his time. During the two centuries since his time, scholars and authorities in education have seen in the humanities the foundation of civilization. The importance of the humanities in enlarging and illuminating one's life cannot be denied. The question remains, however, whether a study of the humanities that embraces the disciplines of philosophy, art, literature, history, and languages builds a commitment to a democratic free society.

This question is also pertinent to the study of the sciences. In our age of technology, the sciences have brought changes of vast dimensions along the whole front of our economy, revolutionized our medical research, and contributed to sweeping changes in the structure of our society. We owe to scientific research great improvements in our health, the greatest industrial productivity known to man, and a knowledge of the laws that govern the universe. But science has also given us weapons that can destroy mankind. The question remains whether the impact of technological change will, on the whole, be for good or for evil and whether these changes will undergird or undermine our commitment to a free self-governing society.

History has not substantiated Jefferson's faith that the study of humanities and of the sciences will safeguard free societies from corruption and despotism. The educational system of pre-World War II Europe, with its sharp division between academic and vocational studies and its concentrated efforts in the humanities and science, did not pass the crucial test of citizenship. The universities, especially, failed in their task of acting as a conscience for society. Those scholars who boasted of their devotion to the causes of truth and culture were silent when intellectual truth and moral freedom were suppressed by the corrupt Nazi regime.

Reinhold Niebuhr, referring to the capitulation of the German universities, wrote, "The culture of the university sought universal truth through the genius of the wise man; and forgot that the wise man is also a sinner, whose interest, passion, and cowardice may corrupt the truth!" (*Beyond Tragedy*, Charles Scribner & Sons, 1937, p. 284.) Curricula concentrating on the humanities or on science only for their own sakes cannot achieve the goal of strengthening our faith in a free society, since knowledge without moral direction becomes aimless and meaningless.

Freedom is not something that can be spoon-fed. It is a state of being that can flourish only when respect for certain basic moral values is instilled not by abstract reasoning or by the accumulation of facts but by recognition of the true values of life, by the hopes and aspirations that govern a nation's destiny and its role in this world of ours.

Professor Jaroslav Pelikan in his lecture "The Individual's Search for Truth—and Its Limitations" emphasizes that the search for truth is itself a moral imperative. In that search, a scholar must be careful to preserve the distinction between end and means. He must also develop his talents to the fullest and take great pains to preserve intellectual honesty. The role of the scholar is a vocation, a calling with its own inherent dignity.

Yet each individual scholar, as Professor Pelikan points out, must operate within a certain array of constraints—some imposed from without, others from within. Most important are the inner restraints that conscience imposes. As Professor Pelikan emphasizes, a special responsibility falls on the philosophers whose task it is to interpret the history and sort out the moral issues of each scholarly field; we need only to witness the great ethical questions recent advances in medicine have brought to the fore to recognize the importance of moral debate in all branches of knowledge.

In the 1993 Lectures on Moral Values in a Free Society, the importance of individual freedom and the danger of self-centeredness are repeatedly stressed, as are the importance of social responsibility and the danger of excessive government control. We must face up to the issues involved both in the exercise of freedom and in its abuse. Social responsibility for the welfare of the nation and of the individual can be discharged without depriving the people of their right to participate freely in the formulation of laws and without the danger of totalitarian tyranny. By exposing injustice and inequality, social conscience keeps before our eyes the ideal of a society based on brotherhood that transforms economic and political relations into fellowship and binds individuals into the human family.

INDIVIDUALISM AND SOCIAL CONSCIENCE

by

Andrew R. Cecil

Andrew R. Cecil

*Andrew R. Cecil is Distinguished Scholar in Residence at
The University of Texas at Dallas. In February 1979 the
University established in his honor the Andrew R. Cecil
Lectures on Moral Values in a Free Society and invited Dr.
Cecil to deliver the first series of lectures in November 1979.
The first annual proceedings were published as Dr. Cecil's
book* The Third Way: Enlightened Capitalism and the
Search for a New Social Order, *which received an enthusi-
astic response. He has also lectured in each subsequent series.
A new book,* The Foundations of a Free Society, *was pub-
lished in 1983.* Three Sources of National Strength *appeared
in 1986, and* Equality, Tolerance, and Loyalty *in 1990. In
1976 the University named for Dr. Cecil the Andrew R. Cecil
Auditorium, and in 1990 it established the Andrew R. Cecil
Endowed Chair in Applied Ethics.*

*Educated in Europe and well launched on a career as a
professor and practitioner in the fields of law and economics,
Dr. Cecil resumed his academic career after World War II in
Lima, Peru, at the University of San Marcos. After 1949, he
was associated with the Methodist church-affiliated colleges
and universities in the United States until he joined The
Southwestern Legal Foundation. Associated with the Foundation since 1958, Dr. Cecil helped guide its development of
five educational centers that offer nationally and interna-
tionally recognized programs in advanced continuing education. Since his retirement as President of the Foundation,
he serves as Chancellor Emeritus and Honorary Trustee.*

*Dr. Cecil is author of fifteen books on the subjects of law,
economics, and religion and of more than seventy articles on
these subjects and on the philosophy of religion published in
periodicals and anthologies. A member of the American Society of International Law, of the American Branch of the
International Law Association, and of the American Judi-
cature Society, Dr. Cecil has served on numerous commis-
sions for the Methodist Church and is a member of the Board
of Trustees of the National Methodist Foundation for Christian Higher Education. In 1981 he was named an Honorary
Rotarian.*

INDIVIDUALISM AND SOCIAL CONSCIENCE

by

Andrew R. Cecil

Individualism grew out of the cultural and intellectual currents of the Renaissance, which from the fourteenth through the sixteenth centuries restored the study of the humanities to a central place in cultural life and fostered the conception of the autonomous, creative individual. The spirit of humanistic individualism centered its interest in the nature, values, possibilities, and self-development of the individual personality. The moral basis of modern individualism, however, must be sought not only in the humanistic tradition of the Renaissance but also in the religious upheaval that accompanied it.

The Impact of Protestantism on Individualism

The emphasis on the individual in the fifteenth and early sixteenth centuries paved the way for the Reformation, the great revolt against the Roman Catholic Church. Out of this revolt came Protestantism, which put emphasis upon the dignity of the individual, who by reason of the doctrine of the priesthood of all believers had inherent rights and privileges. The famous Lutheran declaration of religious freedom proclaimed: "In matters concerning God's honor and the salvation of souls each one must for himself stand before God and give account." The Bible interpreted firsthand by its readers—individual laymen—became the sole arbiter of religious practices and the absolute moral authority, higher than priest, bishop, or pope.

Protestants were revolting against ecclesiastical imperialism by affirming that God is accessible to individual approach. According to Martin Luther, the leader of the Protestant Reformation, God speaks as a voice in the heart of each individual and not through the mediation of the priesthood. The principle that the individual layman could understand "God's Word," with no need of a priest to interpret it for him, lent dignity and worth to those who dissented from certain views and practices of the existing ecclesiastical authority.

It may be noted, however, that the leaders of Protestantism also made highly regrettable blunders in their attitudes toward individual rights. Martin Luther's attempt to suppress the Anabaptist movement was one of the causative factors of the Peasant War of 1524–1525. (The Anabaptists formed the radical wing of the Reformers and advocated far-reaching social and economic reforms.) Luther condemned the peasants' uprising against serfdom as a revolt against civil authority. Luther's conviction that a society should have unequal classes, that "some are free, others captive, some masters, others subjects," and his distrust of merchants and peasants relate to the economic conditions of the sixteenth century. Yet, in spiritual life, Luther in a very real sense stressed the dignity of the individual. Asserting the "priesthood of all believers," he also proclaimed the supreme importance of the individual's relationship with God when he wrote: "God desires to be alone in our consciences, and desires that His word alone should prevail."

John Calvin, who in a similar way argued that "Our consciences have to do, not with men, but with God," was also known for his totalitarian pretensions. He thought that any opposition to the religious practices he advocated constituted an evil that had to be eradicated. For example, Michael Servetus, the Spanish physician and theologian (1511–1553), was condemned by Calvin for his antitrinitarian writings. When some of Servetus' ideas on Christianity were secretly printed, he was investigated by the Inquisition, arrested, tried, and condemned. He escaped from prison, but while making his way to Italy, was seized in Geneva by Calvin's order. After a long trial, he was burned at the stake on October 27, 1553. Yet it should be admitted that from the ideas of some of Calvin's followers—the English Puritans who founded Massachusetts—arose conditions that gave birth to important traditions of American individualism.

Like the Catholics, the early Protestants believed that if a man remained outside their faith he was condemned to burn forever in hell, and therefore he should be compelled even by torture to change his beliefs. Such conversion was deemed to save his soul and provide him with eternal life. In the early days of the Reformation, Lutherans, Calvinists, and other Protestant leaders, claiming a monopoly on truth, tried to silence those whose interpretation of the Holy Scriptures differed from their own. But Protestantism has long since surrendered the idea that religion can be compelled and vested the right and responsibility for religious beliefs in the individual.

In its rebellion against the medieval ecclesiastical control of political and economic as well as spiritual life, Protestantism made a great contribution to the assertion of the importance of individual rights. It originated the separation of church and state and performed an incomparable task in the history of Western civilization by proclaiming the right of the individual to the free exercise of religion and the right to equal opportunities in political, economic, and social life.

Individualism and the Rights of the State

The desire for such individual rights animated the founding of our American republic and produced the Declaration of Independence, the Constitution, and the Bill of Rights. The First Amendment to our Constitution, one of the great pillars of American liberty, states that Congress shall make no law respecting an establishment of religion and provides for freedom of expression. The freedom of belief which is protected from state action includes both the right to speak freely and the right to refrain from speaking. These rights are essential components of a broader concept of freedom of thought; there can be no freedom of thought unless ideas can be uttered.

Those who drafted the Declaration of Independence, the Constitution, and the Bill of Rights offered the individual a broad conception of human freedom and dignity. The religious influences in the framing and adoption of these documents that guaranteed individual rights as the fundamental law of the land should not be ignored or underestimated. We also should not underestimate the impact of the political philosophy that concerned itself with the question of whether there is a conflict between individual rights and responsibilities and society's or the state's rights and responsibilities. This question dominated the thought of prominent philosophers of the seventeenth century, such as Thomas Hobbes (1588–1679) and John Locke (1632–1704).

A. Hobbes

In his chief political work, *Leviathan*, the English philosopher Thomas Hobbes exalted absolute monarchy, stressing the perils of the state of nature that he hypothesized as preceding the formation of political society. According to Hobbes, in the so-called "state of nature" each individual strives for self-preservation and the acquisition of power for the attainment of the ends to which he is naturally impelled. In the nature of man, stated Hobbes, we find three principal causes that lead to a state of war with one another—competition, mistrust, and desire for glory. In this state of war, "force and fraud" are the "cardinal virtues" of individualism. The individual is dependent on his own strength for his security, and "the notions of right and wrong, justice and injustice, have no place."

According to Hobbes, without an organized political society the world would be filled with a multiplicity of human beings, each of whom would use force to obtain pleasure and self-preservation. Only through a social covenant by which men agree to organize a political society and establish a commonwealth can peace by obtained. By this covenant, individuals consent to turn over their rights of self-governance to the sovereign, provided that every member of the prospective society does the same.

The creation of a political society and the selection of a sovereign take place by the same act. Enlightened self-interest calls for concentrating power in the hands of the sovereign, to whom an individual living in a state of anarchy must surrender his selfish rights. Consequently, the sovereign must be supreme, and the individual owes him absolute obedience (although in a very limited number of cases disobedience is justified when the action demanded by the sovereign is contrary to the law of nature).

Hobbes maintained that a breach of the covenant on the part of the sovereign cannot occur because there is no superior power to enforce his compliance. He is not bound by any obligation to the people, and "none of his subjects, by pretense of forfeiture, can be freed from his Subjection." On a similar note, Baruch Spinoza (1632–1677) in his *Tractatus theologico-politicus* asserted that "the sovereign is bound by no law, and that all citizens must obey it in all things."

B. Locke

John Locke's concept of individualism differs from that of Hobbes. Since Locke saw a radical difference between the state of nature and the state of war, he rejected completely Hobbes' concept of the state of nature. In Locke's state of nature, there are natural rights and duties that precede any kind of political organization, since all men are naturally in that state of nature and remain so until by their own consent they make themselves members of some political society.

In Locke's view, the proper state of nature is one in which people live together "according to reason, without a common superior on earth with authority to judge between them...." For Hobbes, natural law meant power, fraud, and force. For Locke, natural law meant the universally accepted moral law recognized by human reason as it reflects on God and on man's relationship to God. This relationship calls for the fundamental equality of all men as creatures endowed with reason. It demands that there be no intrusion on men's rights and no encroachment on their part on the rights of others. These ideas paved the way for the growth of the type of eighteenth-century European individualism known as "enlightened self-interest."

Men, according to Locke, were endowed with certain natural rights even before there was a state. Society was inaugurated by one covenant, and government was established by another that assigned to government the role of a servant of society. The social contract arrived at by people in building their society provides that the role of the government is to preserve peace and protect the rights and liberties of individuals. According to this social contract theory, sovereignty resides in the people, who have the moral right to overthrow a government that does not reflect the popular will. (This right of resistance justified the English "Glorious Revolution" of 1688.) The effective way to restrain lawless despotism is to divide power, so that legislative, judicial, and executive powers are not vested in one man.

Hobbes and Locke differ in their conclusions, but both are individualists in their assumption that individuals play a decisive role in setting up a government to protect themselves and to preserve social order. Their doctrine of social contract gained popularity among churches and religious sects seeking independence from the state's civil power and survived into the eighteenth century.

While in the seventeenth century religious freedom was of supreme importance, in the eighteenth century the primary concerns of those seeking a better society were for freedom of the press, freedom of association, and the right to free elections. Although not all theorists of "social contract" found it historically accurate, and some questioned the very idea that allegiance to government comes from contract as well as the historical reality of the theory (to mention only the Scottish historian and philosopher David Hume, 1711-1776, and the English philosopher Jeremy Bentham, 1748-1832), Locke greatly influenced Thomas Jefferson, and the idea of natural rights of the individual found its expression in our Declaration of Independence. Locke and Jefferson believed that "man, being the workmanship of one omnipotent and infinitely wise Maker," has certain fundamental rights, including those to freedom, food, shelter, and security. Unless these rights are realized, human life is frustrated, if not impossible.

In pointing out the influence of Locke (called the "founder of British Empiricism") on Jefferson, it should also be stressed that the United States' concept of individualism differed greatly from ideological concepts of individualism brought from Europe to America. The broad divergence of these two concepts can be explained by developments in Europe in the eighteenth century and the peculiar structure of democracy in the United States, which was built on two fundamental principles—liberty and equality.

European Individualism

The individualist movement, with its belief in the versatility of man and its emphasis on his desires and abilities, gained prominence—rather deplorable prominence—in the latter part of the eighteenth century with the rise of the Industrial Revolution and industrial capitalism, which appeared in England at the beginning of the 1780s. Adam Smith (1728–1790), who popularized the ideas of free trade and a "natural order" that should not be disturbed by governmental regulation, proclaimed personal freedom and freedom of enterprise as the "obvious and simple system of natural liberty."

Unrestricted economic individualism, as expressed in free trade and free competition, combined with a political individualism that limited governmental interference in private affairs to the protection and maintenance of public order and the enforcement of contracts, caused massive human suffering. This uncontrolled process of a free economy, glorifying extreme "individualism," was characterized by greed, a brutal contempt for human life, and reckless exploitation of men, women, and children. William Blake, the English poet and artist, accused the "dark, satanic mills" of the Industrial Revolution of enslaving man. The term "individualism" in this era meant self-assertion and selfishness, which in its extreme could lead to anarchy. It meant the individual's attachment to his own welfare and near indifference to the social, economic, and political order except as it affected him.

In England, when uncontrolled "individualism" resulted in a monopoly of all economic power in the hands of a few, the wages of workers living in the slums were determined by the so-called "iron law of wages." This law, formulated by the famous British economist David Ricardo, asserted that wages tend to fall to the lowest level acceptable to the most unskilled and desperate worker. In his *Wealth of Nations*, Adam Smith predicted that in the long run wages would be reduced to the lowest level "consistent with common humanity." The lowest level would be determined by "necessaries," which consist of "whatever the custom of the country renders it indecent for creditable people, even of the lowest order, to be without." Labor became a commodity, and the worker was robbed of his dignity and degraded into a dispirited tool of production. Such was the moral expression of European individualism in the early days of the factory system.

The English statesman Edmund Burke (1729–1797) in his *Reflections on the French Revolution* expressed his contempt for individualism by predicting that the commonwealth would "crumble away, be disconnected into the dust and powder of individuality." Obviously Burke used the terms "individualism" and "individuality" interchangeably. In the nineteenth century, individuality gained the positive meaning of a personality attractive by reason of its originality and uniqueness.

American Individualism

European individualism, thus loaded with negative meaning, failed to be transplanted by the immigrants to the United States. The individualism of the pioneers in this country, as we mentioned above, bore very little resemblance to European individualism. This European social and economic individualism—marked by ruthless, self-interested attitudes and by the isolation of individuals from the public and from one another—was transformed in the United States into a loftier, more moral individualism that called for equality of opportunity for each individual, limited government with reliance on self-development, and faith in the dignity and worth of every individual. The pioneers embraced the Jeffersonian ideas of individual rights, self-government, and a democratic free society—ideas that impelled the people of this nation to separate from England.

The American Revolution that began in 1776 was the first historical event of the modern era derived from a belief in individual rights. The Declaration of Independence asserted that human rights could not be abrogated by any human enactment because all men "are endowed by their Creator with certain unalienable rights," namely "Life, Liberty, and the pursuit of Happiness."

Under the doctrine of individual rights, which gained eminence as the greatest of political truths, the term American individualism implied self-confidence, restricted governmental interference in private affairs, and most of all emphasis on the dignity of man and on his moral growth. The self-confidence of the pioneers in this country was fully justified. In their conquest of large areas of a wild continent, they relied on their own determination and unbounded energy. They did not count on the aid of the government or other powers, and since they built their well-being on their own efforts and initiative, they rose in their own esteem and in the respect of others. In their fight for survival they were undergirded by their right to share in the policy decisions that would shape the life of the community in which they lived with no social barriers and none of the irrational discrimination of the "old society."

The settlers, released from the institutions that had evolved in Europe, expected a different world with a different kind of government from the one under which they had lived. In planning the United States as a country where individual rights would be dominant, they restricted governmental action to the narrowest limits. The idea of the limited role of the government could be realized in the kind of environment described by John Adams:

> "In the present state of society and manners in America, with a people living chiefly by agriculture, in small numbers, sprinkled over large tracts of land, they are not subject to those panics and transports, those contagions of madness and folly, which are seen in countries where large numbers live in small places, in daily fear of perishing for want. We know, therefore, that the people can live and increase *under almost any kind of government, or without any government at all.*" (*Defense of the Constitutions of Government of the United States* in *The Works of John Adams*, Vol. IV, Little and Brown, 1851, p. 587. Emphasis added.)

In the new republic the binding power of the majority was predominant. The question arose whether the obligation to conform with the decision of the majority might lead to tyranny of the majority. Alexis de Tocqueville, the celebrated author of *Democracy in America*, warned:

> "If ever freedom is lost in America, that will be due to the omnipotence of the majority driving the minorities to desperation and forcing them to appeal to physical force. We may then see anarchy, but it will come as the result of despotism." (Ed. by J. P. Mayer and Max Lerner, Harper & Row, 1966, p. 240.)

Tocqueville's concern proved to be ill-founded. The constitutional provisions concerning the balance of powers, the deeply vested belief in individual rights, and the religiously based expectation that the government adhere to generally accepted moral principles vested sovereignty in the people and not in the majority. Tocqueville himself dispelled his fear that the rule of the majority could turn into legal tyranny when he defined the dogma of the sovereignty of the people in the United States:

> "In the United States the dogma of the sovereignty of the people is not an isolated doctrine, bearing no relation to the people's habits and prevailing ideas; . . . Providence has given each individual the amount of reason necessary for him to look after himself in matters of his own exclusive concern. That is the great maxim on which civil and political society in the United States rests; the father of a family applies it to his children, a master to his servants, a township to those under its administration, a province to the townships, a state to the provinces, and the Union to the states. Extended to the nation as a whole, it becomes the dogma of the sovereignty of the people." (*Id.*, p. 364.)

Consequently Tocqueville saw no danger of the republican principles' perishing in the United States nor any reason to foresee a revolution against them and "no symptom indicat[ing] its approach." (*Ibid.*)

A. *The Dignity of Man*

The individual's regal place in the creation of this world was recorded by the Psalmist in his memorable answer to the question: What is man that the Lord is mindful of him?

> "For thou hast made him a little lower than the angels, and hast crowned him with glory and honour. Thou madest him to have dominion over the works of thy hands; thou hast put all things under his feet:" (Psalm 8: 5-6)

The sovereignty of the people can succeed only under conditions where morality goes hand in hand with public policy and where faith in the worth and dignity of every individual gains popular support. In this country, the commitment to protect and defend the dignity and sacredness of the individual personality has a rich tradition, which dates back to the Massachusetts Body of Liberties of 1641. That document provides that

> "No man's life shall be taken away, no man's honor or good name shall be stayned, no man's person shall be arrested . . . no man's goods or estate shall be taken away from him . . . unless it be by virtue or equitie of some express law of the country. . . ."

Our forefathers' individualism focused on the opportunity of each individual to make his own place in society, with none excluded by birth from access to political power. Their idea of individual rights stressed equality of opportunity in all areas of life as the unalienable birthright of every person, lifting men from rags to riches, from the log cabin to the White House. Individual status depended not on inherited but on achieved qualities.

This country was built on a spiritual foundation that proclaimed that a person is more than a political pawn enjoying only the privileges bestowed upon him by the state. In the new republic molded by the quest for liberty, persons were not regarded as economic expendables or commodities; they deserved maximum opportunity for the development of their individual personalities. American individualism did not expect the individual to isolate himself from the society in which he lived. On the contrary, individuals had a sacred obligation to make every possible effort to enable others to live in decency. Exclusive concern with personal gain and selfishness that violates the moral principle of love for one's fellowman were, therefore, condemned.

The concept of the dignity of the individual, which was the moving force guiding the founders of this country, represented the heritage of their religious faith. Our forefathers combined personal independence with carrying out the ideas emanating from the Old and New Testaments of service to the poor and the handicapped, of tolerance based on the belief in the sanctity of the individual, and of moral authority transcending all offices and boundaries. These beliefs enable people to live together despite the differences that divide them. The settlers, always relying on their own efforts rather than aid from other sources, were also ready to help in harvesting the crops of a neighbor incapacitated by illness or in restoring his barn destroyed by fire.

B. *Individualism and the Common Good*

One of the chapters of *Democracy in America* deals with the principle of self-interest properly understood. Tocqueville describes "individualism" as "a word recently coined to express a new idea. Our fathers knew only about egoism." He defines individualism as "a calm and considered feeling which disposes each citizen to isolate himself from the mass of his fellows and withdraw into the circle of family and friends; with this little society formed to his taste, he gladly leaves the greater society to look after itself." Having identified individualism with egoism, Tocqueville points out the perils of the latter: "Egoism sterilizes the seeds of every virtue; individualism at first only dams the spring of public virtues, but in the long run it attacks and destroys all the others too and finally merges in egoism." (*Id.*, p. 477.)

In his chapter "How the Americans Combat the Effects of Individualism by Free Institutions," Tocqueville, who like John Stuart Mill feared paternalistic government that might lead to oppression by the state, stresses the special character of American individualism, in which "each man notices that he is not as independent of his fellows as he used to suppose and that to get their help he must often offer his aid to them." (*Id.*, p. 481.) He remarks that he has often seen Americans "make really great sacrifices for the common good, and I have noticed a hundred cases in which, when help was needed, they hardly ever failed to give each other trusty support." (*Id.*, pp. 483-484.) He makes a revealing observation that an American sacrifices himself for his fellowman not because it is a virtue to do so, but because such sacrifice is as necessary for the man who makes it as for the beneficiaries. In their concern for their fellowman, the Americans are "carried away by the disinterested, spontaneous impulses natural to man." It gives them pleasure, wrote Tocqueville, to point out how "an enlightened self-love continually leads them to help one another and disposes them freely to give part of their time and wealth for the good of the state." (*Id.*, p. 498.)

This faith in the greatness of the individual was expressed beautifully by Walt Whitman:

> "I swear I begin to see the meaning of these things!
> . . . it is not America who is so great,
> It is not I who am so great or to be great, it is You
> up there, or any one;
> It is to walk rapidly through civilizations,
> governments, theories,
> Through poems, pageants, shows, to form
> individuals.
> Underneath all, individuals . . .
> The American compact is altogether with
> individuals. . . ." ("By Blue Ontario's Shore,"
> ll. 250-257, in *Leaves of Grass*, ed. by Harold W.
> Blodgett and Sculley Bradley, New York University Press, 1965, p. 352.)

Our social, economic, and political systems, which give the individual the opportunity to achieve his or her maximum potential, are also entrusted with the responsibility for advancing the welfare of all citizens. The success of our national life depends on our voluntary efforts to seek our fellowman's satisfaction in the realm of material as well as spiritual needs.

Conscience as the Norm of Morality

The American concept of individualism, which relates not only to the interests of a particular person but also to "the good of the state," reflects the nature of an American national conscience that determines the social and moral ideas of our society. We shall limit our discussion to the manner in which our laws and jurisprudence are molded in response to the compelling sentiments and demands of this common conscience, of the common sense of right and wrong. But first, let us try to define the term "conscience."

In the fourteenth century, the Franciscan theologian and philosopher William of Ockham, who contended that the emperor and not the pope should have complete authority in all temporal matters, offered two moral theories in his *Sentences*. The first, presented by Ockham in his capacity as a theologian, accepts the existence of a moral order revealed in Christianity. The second, presented in his capacity as a philosopher, was greatly influenced by Aristotle's ethical teachings about "right reason", or conscience, as the norm of morality. Ockham, like Aristotle, believed that it is man's duty to follow his conscience, even if it is an erroneous one, as long as he in good faith believes it to be right. (According to Aristotle, it is possible for a man following his erroneous conscience to be in "invincible ignorance" and thus not responsible for his error.)

Because of the manifold and often contradictory connotations of the word "conscience," the German Lutheran theologian Richard Rothe (1799-1867), who saw a close connection between religion and ethics, suggested that this term should be excluded from the scientific treatment of ethics. Conscience, however, plays such an important part in determining the role and scope of morality in public life that we cannot escape from trying to consider what it is and what its function should be. According to some philosophers, conscience connotes a form of intuition that gives us the power to distinguish between right and wrong.

To the British philosopher Anthony Cooper, Lord Shaftesbury (1671-1713), is attributed the term "moral sense"—man's natural sense of right and wrong in a universe which is essentially harmonious. He saw no conflict between man's natural ideas for happiness and well-being and the need for the welfare of society as a whole. His ideas were followed by Francis Hutcheson (1694–1746), a professor of moral philosophy at the University of Glasgow, who in his "benevolent theory" of moral conduct argued that the satisfaction from virtuous and benevolent behavior arises not from the benefits it brings to the one who practiced it but from the beauty and merits of the act itself. Shaftesbury, Hutcheson, and other philosophers maintained that moral ideas are innate in man, that man possesses an "inborn sense" that enables him to discern moral values. They therefore rejected Hobbes' interpretation, described above, of man as selfish, guided only by the "cardinal virtues" of force and fraud to obtain self-preservation.

The inner perception of conscience was regarded as important by the moral philosophers known as intuitionists. Foremost among them was the German metaphysician Immanuel Kant (1724-1804), who in his revolutionary metaphysical system accepted a universal moral law as pragmatically necessary. According to Kant, the moral imperative is absolute, and the moral sense is innate, not derived from questionable individual experience.

Opposed to this idea of an innate moral sense by which each person distinguishes between right and wrong is the empiricists' theory that there is no innate moral faculty as such but that all our knowledge comes from experience and through our senses. John Locke denied the existence of innate ideas inherent in the mind from birth, inborn in every human soul. He taught that each man enters the world not equipped with ideas but with a mind that is a clean sheet—a *tabula rasa*. Sense-experience begets ideas of right and wrong, and moral judgment comes from man's experience and his voluntary actions with regard to human or divine law. Thus, such judgments may vary with geography and over historical time. Conscience, according to Locke and the empiricists, is not innate but acquired.

The English philosopher Herbert Spencer (1820-1903) tried to reconcile the two conflicting theories. By applying Darwin's principle of evolution to the realm of morals, he maintained that conscience, like everything else, has evolved through the process of adaptation to the ends of life, and thus has become the product of age-long experience. But Spencer also admitted that certain moral conceptions may have become hereditary with individuals. Spencer reconciled the theories of the intuitionists and the empiricists by accepting the belief that there is an inborn moral sense, as well as the ideas of those representing the new evolutionary view.

National Conscience

I discussed at some length the concept of conscience in my book *The Foundations of a Free Society* (The University of Texas at Dallas, 1983, pp. 36-48). In our current discussion of the impact of national conscience on our laws and jurisprudence, it will be helpful to bring out three observations.

First, conscience is governed by no man-made laws and is unaccountable to human tribunals. St. Thomas Aquinas (1225–1274) asserted the autonomy of the individual in the sphere of conscience by stating that everyone "is bound to examine his own actions according to the knowledge which he has from God." (*Questiones disputatae de veritate*, qu. 17, art. 4, in *Truth*, trans. by James V. McGlynn, Henry Regnery Companny, 1953, p. 337.) Conscience is the result of judgment tested by reason and yields to the decision of an intelligent mind in approving or condemning man's or society's actions.

Second, the moral sense may differ in degree in individual members of society and in different societies, but no reasonable being, whether controlled by it or not in his conduct, is wholly destitute of it. As conscience was once described by our courts: "Greatly enlightened it is in some by reason of superior education, quickened in others because of settled religious belief in future accountability, dulled in others by vicious habits, but never altogether absent in any." (*Miller v. Miller*, 41 A. 277, 280, 187 Pa. 572 [1898].)

Third, in our discussion we use interchangeably the terms national conscience, social conscience, and the community's *mores*. National conscience is a broad term; no definition will cover all the concepts allied with it. The commonly accepted meaning is adherence to generally prevailing standards of right conduct that enhance a nation's well-being. This meaning, we realize, is not sufficiently definite or inclusive. No more inclusive or definite is the theory of the "general will," which the French revolutionist, Emanuel Joseph, Abbe Sieyes (1748-1836), referred to as the "national will." This concept may be akin to the term "national conscience." Charles de Montesquieu (1689-1755) saw in the legislative power the "general will (*volonté general*) of the state," while the role of the executive power was the execution of the general will. The French philosopher Denis Diderot (1713-1784) saw in the general will the universal bond obliging mankind.

The general will, argued Jean-Jacques Rousseau (1712-1778)—the most frequently quoted thinker of eighteenth-century France—is the voice of the people, in fact the voice of God (*vox populi, vox dei*). He believed that individuals, by surrendering their power over themselves to the people as a whole, would create an infallible sovereignty that would act by the dictates of the general will. The important role of a legitimate and popular government, according to Rousseau, is "to follow in everything the general will" and the "first duty of the legislator is to make the law comformable to the general will."

Among the German philosophers, Friedrich Hegel (1770-1831), one of the most influential thinkers of the nineteenth century, saw in the state, created by historical forces emanating from the interaction of the individual and society, the institution expressive of the mind of the nation and of its moral life. Mankind's development, according to Hegel, led to the creation of the state as a historical necessity, and therefore the citizen who respects the law is free since the law of the state is the expression of the essential, universal nature of the human spirit. Political developments that occurred much later (such as communism, fascism, and Nazism), as well as the manifest fallibility of legislators even in democratic countries, have not verified Hegel's and Rousseau's theories.

As we mentioned above, Immanuel Kant believed that a moral law providing universally valid rules of conduct was pragmatically necessary. Kant called the supreme moral principle which man ought to follow the "categorical imperative," the unconditional demand of the conscience: "Act as if the maxim from which you act were to become through your will a universal law of nature." This brings us back to the concept of conscience.

All three observations described above as pertinent to our discusssion of the impact of conscience on our laws and on the administration of justice characterize conscience as the inner convictions that lead to the fulfillment of man's moral duties. The word "moral" derives from the Latin word *mores*, which means the accepted standards of traditional human behavior. In referring to a "national conscience," we seek to describe the moral standards of traditional behavior of a people living in common territorial boundaries and with a common heritage, not a state with its government's undisputed authority. This distinction is important when we are reminded of George Washington's warning that nations—with the apparatus of the state at their disposal—in their proverbial selfishness were not to be trusted beyond their own interest.

It should also be noted that there may sometimes appear to be a conflict between the imperatives of the individual's conscience and the needs of society. Reinhold Niebuhr, the prominent theologian and late professor of Christian ethics at Union Theological Seminary, points out in his book *Moral Man and Immoral Society* the conflict between individual and social morality. From the perspective of society, the highest moral ideal is justice, while from the perspective of the individual the highest ideal is unselfishness. The two moral perspectives, writes Professor Niebuhr, "are not mutually exclusive and the contradiction between them is not absolute. But neither are they easily harmonized." (Charles Scribner's Sons, New York, 1960, p. 257.) We shall make an effort to harmonize these two concepts of morality. But first let me try to elaborate upon the role of national conscience in defining "the highest moral ideal" of justice by its impact on our laws and the administration of justice.

A. Legislation and the Mores of the Community

To follow the rule of law does not imply that the law always fulfills our notions of the dictates of the accepted mores of the community. There are moral claims and duties, comprehended under the promptings of humanity, benevolence, or charity, which law does not enforce; their fulfillment is left to man's conscience and honor. Experience also shows that the law is not always accepted as moral by an enlightened public opinion, nor does it always punish or restrain some violations of existing moral standards. It is not surprising, therefore, that there is no agreement among legal scholars as to whether law and morals are separate modes of social control or whether they are to be made identical by conforming legal precepts to the requirements of right conduct that find their expression in a reasoned system of morals.

The historical school of the interpretation of law saw in historic experience a substitute for the standard of "right reason," with no need for conformity to *a priori* principles of right and justice such as those offered by the doctrine of natural law. In other words, law in its historical growth should express the morality of the community it serves—morality that develops unconsciously from one age to another. Law should thus express the ethical and moral principles that move forward under the dynamics of human history.

In Germany, Frederick Karl von Savigny (1779–1861), one of the foremost jurists of his age and one of the earliest adherents to the tenets of the historical school, denied in his great work *On the Call of Our Time for Legislation and Science of Law* (1814) the efficacy of legal codes and reforms alien to the people they have to serve. Like Hume and Bentham, he did not believe in natural law or any other absolute. Law, according to Savigny, "takes actual life as its starting point." It reflects the spirit of the people as expressed in their manners and customs. What creates the relationship between social phenomena and legal concepts "is the common conviction of the people, the kindred consciousness of an inward necessity *excluding all notions of an accidental and arbitrary origin.*" [Emphasis added.] The essence of Savigny's conception of law as something realized as a result of a process of silent growth and of a customary morality that develops unconsciously from one age to another was also expressed by Justice Oliver Wendell Holmes when he wrote in *The Common Law*:

"The life of the law has not been logic: it has been experience. The felt necessities of the time, the prevalent moral and political theories, intuitions of public policy, avowed or unconscious, even the prejudices which judges share with their fellow-men have had a good deal more to do than the syllogism in determining the rules by which men should be governed." (*The Common Law*, Little, Brown and Company, 1963, p. 5.)

The final cause and end of the law is to serve society. Statutes, therefore, are not to be viewed in isolation but should remain in harmony with present-day conditions and opinions generally prevailing in the community they serve. Opinions are shaped by history as well as by logic, customs, and ethical considerations. It is indispensable that a law conform to the moral requirements dictated by the community in a given stage of its development if it is to meet its objective and pass the test of promoting fundamental social interests. If a law, after it has been tested by experience, is found to be inconsistent with these moral requirements, it loses its reason for existing and should be abandoned.

The rules of law that guide one generation may be discarded by another upon the discovery of a new sense of justice or a new concept of social well-being. As Holmes expressed it, "The law is the witness and external deposit of our moral life. Its history is the history of the moral development of the race." (*Path of the Law*, 10 Harvard Law Review 457, 466 [1897].) In our generation we have witnessed dramatic changes in rules of law that have occurred in response to the development of a new customary morality, to mention only the areas of civil rights, labor, and antitrust legislation.

To realize the legal impact of new conditions that

bring about changing moral standards, it is helpful to compare the "three compromises" found in the Constitution with the civil rights legislation of the last three decades. In Article I, Section 2, it was provided that three-fifths of the slaves were to be counted in assessing taxes and in ascertaining how many members a state should have in the House of Representatives; Section 9 of Article I postponed abolition of the slave trade for twenty years (until 1808); Section 2 of Article IV was designed to assure the slave-holding states that slaves who might flee to northern states would not become free.

The Thirteenth Amendment and paragraph 2 of the Fourteenth corrected the slavery provisions of the original Constitution. The purpose of the Equal Protection Clause (paragraph 1 of the Fourteenth Amendment) was to ensure that no state could abridge the rights of citizens of the United States, and paragraph 5 provided the basis for federal enforcement legislation. A number of such statutes were passed from 1865 to 1875. Several Presidents sought to curtail discrimination by issuing Executive Orders. The first in this century was issued by President Franklin D. Roosevelt to create the Fair Employment Practices Commission. But these orders lacked adequate means of enforcement.

The civil rights legislation of the last three decades—to mention only the Civil Rights Act of 1964, the Voting Rights Act of 1965, and the Civil Rights Act of 1992—and numerous federal regulations and state laws were designed to eliminate discrimination. These, along with the current array of legal measures to promote equal employment opportunity, offer more effective and farther reaching remedies against the barriers of discrimination based on race, sex, age, creed, and physical handicap than were previously available to enforce the Equal Protection Clause in this respect.

Under the impact of new concepts of social well-being, labor laws enacted around the turn of this century were abandoned in the wake of the New Deal, the Fair Deal, and the Great Society. A century ago there was little legislation dealing with labor unions. The law held unions to be a harmful, if not dangerous, type of association with antisocial aims. The courts applied the common law and particularly its doctrines of conspiracy and restraint of trade to put unionists in jail. They recognized the validity of "yellow dog" contracts, by which workers promised not to join a union, and freely used injunctions against labor. Such injunctions were used extensively to defeat strikes.

The Sherman Antitrust Act of 1890, which made monopolistic restraints of trade illegal, was also used by the courts to curb the activities of the unions. Although the Clayton Act of 1914 exempted union activities from the antitrust laws, judicial opposition to the labor movement continued. The courts' adverse decisions with penalties in the form of prison sentences and fines often ruined the unions.

The legislators and the courts, feeling the power of society's moral norms, gave up denouncing the unions when they realized that no law can survive after it has become out of harmony with the social views of the people. During the 1930s the pendulum swung in favor of labor. The Norris-La Guardia Act of 1932 outlawed yellow-dog contracts and practically wiped out the power of the courts to issue injunctions in labor disputes. The National Labor Relations Act of 1935 (the Wagner

Act) enumerated unfair labor practices affecting employees and provided that employees have the right to organize, to bargain collectively through representatives of their own choosing, and to engage in concerted activities for mutual aid or protection. Moreover, it established the National Labor Relations Board to protect employees from employers' "unfair labor practices." These provisions of the Wagner Act succeeded in encouraging the growth of labor unions.

Other legislation during the Roosevelt administration heightened the advantages of organized labor. The Social Security Act of 1935 provided unemployment insurance or compensation, contributory old-age benefits, and noncontributory old-age and handicapped group assistance. The Fair Labor Standards Act of 1938 (known as the "Wage-Hour" law) established the minimum wage, later gradually raised, and reduced the work week to forty hours.

After World War II, the pendulum went in reverse. The 1947 Labor-Management Relations Act (known as the "Taft-Hartley Act") was an attempt to restore some equilibrium in employer-employee relations. It included a list of unfair practices of unions. Although the labor unions attacked the act as unfair to labor, the union movement was not crippled, and the list of unfair labor practices of employers was retained.

Also because of changing moral standards, the almost unrestrained enjoyment of the use of property and of economic liberty, which in the past century characterized our system, has disappeared. In response to an irresistible tide of public opinion, the Sherman Act, the Clayton Act, the Federal Trade Commission Act, and the Robinson-Patman Act were aimed at practices con-

sidered dangerous to trade and commerce. Their
purpose was to clamp down on mergers that might sub-
stantially lessen competition and to arrest a trend
toward centralization in its incipiency before the trend
developed to the point that a market was left in the grip
of a monopoly.

All of the developments we have been discussing—
civil rights and labor legislation, antidiscriminatory
measures such as the Fair Housing and Equal Employment Opportunity Acts and affirmative action, as well as
developments in other areas, such as environmental
regulation, have changed the concepts of individual
rights, property, free enterprise, and liberty embodied
in our past laws.

In evaluating the impact of changing mores on legislation, we should point out that social conscience demands that the law be impartial. There seems to be no
consensus whether the elimination of prior discrimination, for instance, justifies another kind of state-enforced
discrimination favoring the promotion of a woman or a
member of a minority group over a male or white employee with a higher test score. The goal of proportionate
representation by race and sex in the workplace gave
rise to the issue of quotas, which has been widely discussed in election campaigns. Discrimination in reverse
is not a solution, because two wrongs do not make a right,
but there is no doubt that in response to the voice of
national conscience we have made enormous progress in
enacting laws enhancing equality and trying to remedy
the imbalance reflecting underrepresentation of women
and minority groups in the job market.

B. The Administration of Justice and the Mores of the Community

Justice Benjamin Cardozo, defining judgment as "a process of discovery, and not in any degree a process of creation," described his conception of law

> "as a body of rules and principles and standards which in their extension to new combinations of events are to be sorted, selected, molded, and adapted in subordination to an end. A process of trial and error brings judgments into being. A process of trial and error determines their rights to reproduce their kind." (*Growth of the Law*, in *Selected Writings of Benjamin Nathan Cardozo*, edited by Margaret E. Hall, Matthew Bender & Co., 1947, pp. 208–209.)

Just as the history of our legislation gives evidence that accepted standards of moral conduct shape the progress of the law, we can trace the similar impact that changing standards have had on the decisions of our courts. According to the American jurist John Forrest Dillon, "Ethical considerations can no more be excluded from the administration of justice which is the end and purpose of all civil laws than one can exclude the vital air from this room and live." (*The Laws and Jurisprudence of England and America*, quoted in *Selected Writings of Benjamin Nathan Cardozo*, p. 133.)

The cardinal principles of justice are immutable, but the methods by which justice is administered are subject to fluctuations. Each generation originates important reforms that draw their inspiration from new experi-

ences, from the progress and broadened vision of society,
and from advancement of legal and social sciences. The
tide of social change reflects the standard of what, in a
free society at a given time, is deemed reasonable and
right. These standards do not become petrified as of any
one time. The courts are expected to give full consideration to the changing standards and conditions developing in a free society.

Only some rights have the quality of eternal verity,
while others cannot be confined within a permanent
catalogue of the essential, fundamental rights. The
administration of justice by our courts requires close and
perceptive inquiry into the directions in which the tide of
social change has turned—always with due regard to the
landmarks established for the protection of citizens and
their security. The administration of justice, as Justice
Felix Frankfurter explained, is based upon the conscience of society, ascertained as best may be by a tri-
bunal disciplined for the task and "environed by the best
safeguards for disinterestedness and detachment."

A right so fundamental that it has "eternal verity" is
the right to due process of law enshrined in the Fifth and
Fourteenth Amendments to the Constitution. Both
amendments command that no person shall be deprived
"of life, liberty, or property without due process of law."
In my book *The Foundations of a Free Society*, I listed
due process of law as one of those foundations. (*Id.*, pp.
105–154.) To avoid repetitiveness, let me only mention
that the due process clause is founded on the essential
nature of individual rights, which are not limited to life,
liberty, or property. It safeguards also our inherent
rights, indispensable to the existence of a free society
and protected by the general standards of fairness and
decency.

The due process clause, and consequently the courts that are called to interpret it, are not imprisoned within the limits of any formula with a fixed content unrelated to varying circumstances. The remedies offered by the due process clause as applied by the courts may change from time to time since the very nature of this clause negates any inflexibility. The facts and circumstances of each case may vary, but the purpose of due process of law and the concomitant responsibility for the impartial administration of justice never vary: Both must resist any encroachment upon the rights of the individual and avoid any unfairness resulting from the use of powers which the state may exercise.

Due process of law, according to Justice Frankfurter, requires in each case an evaluation based on a disinterested inquiry pursued in the spirit of science, on a balanced order of facts exactly and fairly stated, on detached consideration of conflicting claims, on a judgment not *ad hoc* and episodic but duly mindful of the duty to reconcile the needs both of continuity and of change in a progressive society. (*Rochin v. California*, 342 U.S. 165, 172, 72 S.Ct. 205, 209 [1951]). On a similar note, Justice Cardozo, referring to decisions under the due process clause, described it as a summarized constitutional guarantee of respect for those personal immunities which are "so rooted in the tradition and conscience of our people as to be ranked as fundamental." (*Snyder v. Massachusetts*, 291 U.S. 97, 105, 54 S.Ct. 330, 332 [1933].)

For Justice Cardozo, "every judgment has a generative power. . . . It is charged with vital power. It is a source from which new principles or norms may spring to shape sentences thereafter." Although he sees in *stare decisis* "at least the everyday working rule of our law," he acknowledges "the propriety of relaxing the rule in exceptional conditions." (*The Nature of the Judicial Process*, in *Selected Writings*, pp. 112–113.)

What are these "exceptional conditions"? These are the changes that constantly occur in our dynamic society— economic, social, and political—that create new demands that have an impact on the courts' administration of justice. Because of these demands, the principle of adhering to precedent, which offers continuity with the past and attempts to guarantee that all people will be treated alike, no longer satisfies our society's expectation that the judicial process should be adapted to varying conditions. The United States Supreme Court has explicitly asserted the right to overrule a prior constitutional decision when it realizes that it is wrong.

Court decisions that, after they have been duly tested by experience and society's "moral sense," have been found inconsistent with new conditions and society's conscience are destined for abandonment. French jurists advocate the judicial interpretation of statutes in "le sense evolutif" that calls for inquiring what the legislator would have willed if he had known what the new conditions would be.

Precedents must be discarded or modified when they become inconsistent with new rules of conduct and changes in the fundamental desires of the society. The use of precedents, or the principle of *stare decisis*, must give way before the compelling force of the society's moral and ethical principles that form its conscience.

Broadly speaking, the administration of justice has to satisfy a sense of fairness through a process of continued adjustment involving the exercise of judgment based on experience of the past, sound reason, an unfailing belief in the sacredness of human rights, and the conscience of the people—which we have called the national conscience. To avoid high-sounding rhetoric, let us illustrate the impact of social conscience on the administration of justice by selecting some of the cases from the great number brought before the Supreme Court on the ground that prior Court decisions are inconsistent with new conditions and changed moral standards. In the light of a rising new sense of fairness, prior constitutional decisions have been declared wrong because they violated individual rights guaranteed by the Constitution. They called for conduct that did not conform to the common moral standards of society.

Let us start with the dramatic changes that took place in Supreme Court decisions concerning segregation. In the 1857 case of *Dred Scott v. John F. A. Stanford,* which foreshadowed the crisis of the Civil War, Chief Justice Roger Taney declared that it was the intention of the authors of the Constitution to perpetuate an "impassable barrier" between the white race and the whole "enslaved African race." The Court concluded that Negroes are "altogether unfit to associate with the white race, either in social or political relations and so far inferior, that they had no rights which the white man was bound to respect. . . ." (19 How. 393–638, 15 L. Ed. 691 [1857].)

Forty years later, in 1896, the U.S. Supreme Court in the case of *Plessy v. Ferguson* adopted the doctrine of "separate but equal" by taking the position that the object of the Fourteenth Amendment was not to abolish distinction based upon color or to enforce social (as distinguished from political) equality or the "commingling of two races upon terms unsatisfactory to either." The Court suggested that legislatures were powerless to eradicate racial instincts, and "if one race is inferior to the other socially, the Constitution of the United States cannot put them on the same plane." (163 U.S. 537 [1896].)

In 1954, more than a half century later, the Supreme Court held in the case of *Brown v. Board of Education of Topeka* that segregation of children in public schools solely on the basis of race, even though the physical facilities and other tangible factors might be equal, deprived the children of the minority group of equal educational opportunities in contravention of the Equal Protection Clause of the Fourteenth Amendment. The Court concluded that in the field of public education the doctrine of "separate but equal" has no place, because "we cannot turn the clock . . . to 1896 when *Plessy v. Ferguson* was written. We must consider public education in the light of its full development and its present place in American life throughout the Nation." (347 U.S. 492 [1954].)

Decisions are reversed as our perception of justice and natural rights develops. There was no need for a half century to elapse (as occurred in segregation cases) for the Supreme Court to reverse its previous constitutional decisions. Within a three-year period the Court did a complete about-face by changing its position on the constitutionality of state requirements of the flag salute.

In 1935 the School Board of the Minersville public schools promulgated a regulation that required all teachers and pupils of those schools to salute the flag of the United States as a part of daily exercises. Refusal to salute the flag was regarded as an act of insubordination. When Lilian Gobitis, age twelve, and her brother William, age ten, as Jehovah's Witnesses, refused to salute the flag on the grounds that the Scripture forbade bowing down to a graven image (Exodus 20:4–5), they were expelled from the public schools. A federal district court enjoined the school district from prohibiting the attendance of the two children at the Minersville public schools.

The United States Court of Appeals for the Third Circuit affirmed the decree of the district court. The regulation promulgated by the school board, in the opinion of the Court of Appeals, was an unconstitutional infringement on the free exercise of religion as applied to pupils who conscientiously object to saluting the flag on religious grounds.

In 1940, on appeal the Supreme Court reversed the decision of the Court of Appeals (*Minersville School District v. Gobitis*, 310 U.S. 586, 60 S. Ct. 609 [1940]. Justice Felix Frankfurter, speaking for the eight-man majority, stressed that the mere possession of religious convictions which contradict the relevant concerns of a political society does not relieve the citizen from the discharge of political responsibilities. The ultimate foundation of a free society is the binding tie of cohesive sentiment, and the flag salute is one of the means to evoke the unifying sentiment "without which there can ultimately be no liberties, civil or religious."

Three years later in the case of *West Virginia State Board of Education v. Barnette* (319 U.S. 624, 53 S. Ct. 1178, [1943] Justice Jackson's majority opinion overruled the *Gobitis* decision, and two justices of the *Gobitis* majority (Black and Douglas) made the unusual admission that the *Gobitis* case was wrongly decided.

Justice Jackson rejected the proposition that national unity was the question in the flag-salute controversy.

The problem was, he stated, whether under our Constitution compulsion as employed by the board of education was a permissible means of achieving such unity. Referring to efforts by totalitarian countries to compel coherence as a means to unity, Justice Jackson concluded: "Compulsory unification of opinion achieves only the unanimity of the graveyard." (For a more extensive discussion of the flag controversy see pp. 93–107 of my book, *Three Sources of National Strength*, University of Texas at Dallas, 1986.)

Finally, closer to our time, the U.S. Supreme Court passed on the constitutionality of state statutes regulating abortion in *Roe v. Wade* (410 U.S. 113 [1973]), the landmark case of our generation. *Roe v. Wade* held that the constitutional right of privacy protects absolutely a woman's decision to terminate her pregnancy in the first trimester, provided only that the abortion be performed by a licensed physician. The decision, which marked a revolutionary change in the law, inspired a raging debate and became the subject of heated controversy in political campaigns.

One point of view (pro-choice) asserts that a woman has the sole right to do with her body as she sees fit. Furthermore, when women defy the law in desperation, placing their health and safety in the hands of "back-alley" abortionists or attempting to perform abortions on themselves, the results can be disastrous.

The other point of view (pro-life) argues that life begins at conception and is present throughout pregnancy, and that therefore the state has a compelling interest in protecting life from and after conception. This interest goes beyond the protection of the pregnant woman alone; the state's interest and general obligation extends to prenatal life. Since human life begins with conception, abortion is murder. From the U.S. Supreme Court decisions dealing with the constitutionality of state statutes enacting restrictive antiabortion regulations (to mention only *Maher v. Roe*, 97 S. Ct. 2376 [1977]; *Poelker v. Doe*, 97 S. Ct. 2391, 2392 [1977]; *Harris v. McRae*, 100 S. Ct. 3040 [1980]; and *Planned Parenthood v. Casey*, 112 S.Ct. 2791 [1992]), we single out *Webster v. Reproductive Health Services* (109 S. Ct. 3040 [1989]), which limited considerably a woman's right to decide whether to terminate pregnancy.

In the *Webster* case, state-employed health care professionals and facilities offering abortion counseling and services challenged the constitutionality of the Missouri statute regulating the performance of abortions. Under the *Roe v. Wade* framework, the state may not fully regulate abortion in the interest of potential life of the fetus (as opposed to maternal health) until the third trimester. (State involvement in second trimester abortions is limited to protecting maternal health.)

The Missouri statute requires that prior to performing an abortion on any woman whom a physician has reason to believe is twenty or more weeks pregnant, the physician must ascertain whether the fetus is viable by performing "such medical examinations and tests as are necessary to make a finding of the gestational age, weight, and lung maturity of the unborn child."

The act also prohibits the use of public employees and facilities to perform or assist abortions not necessary to save the mother's life and it prohibits the use of public funds, employees, or facilities for the purpose of "encouraging or counseling" a woman to have an abortion not necessary to save her life.

Chief Justice Rehnquist delivered the opinion, con-
cluding that none of the challenged provisions of the
Missouri act described above were in conflict with the
Constitution. The opinion of Chief Justice Rehnquist, in
which he was joined by Justices White and Kennedy,
pointed out in part IID that "*stare decisis* is a cornerstone
of our legal system, but it has less power in constitutional
cases, where, save for constitutional amendments, the
Court is the only body able to make needed changes."

In the opinion of the three Justices, the key elements of
the *Roe* framework—trimesters and viability—are not
found in the text of the Constitution or in any place else
one would expect to find a constitutional principle. Consequently, the Court should not refrain from reconsideration of a prior construction of the Constitution that has
proved "unsound in principle and unworkable in
practice" and should abandon the *Roe* trimester framework. (109 S.Ct. Reporter 3040, 3056 [1989]. Justices
Scalia and O'Connor, making up the 5-to-4 plurality with
the three justices mentioned above, concurred with the
judgment but declined to concur with the opinion, although for totally opposite reasons.)

As to the use of public facilities and staff, the Court
stated that nothing in the Constitution requires states to
enter or remain in the business of performing abortions.
Nor do private physicians and their patients have some
kind of constitutional right of access to public facilities to
perform abortions. According to Justice Scalia, who
concurred with the judgment, the *Webster* decision effectively overruled *Roe v. Wade*, but in his opinion, it
should have been done "more explicitly." (In *Planned
Parenthood v. Casey* Chief Justice Rehnquist and Justices White and Thomas also argued that the *Roe* de-

cision can and should be overruled "consistently with our traditional approach to *stare decisis* in constitutional cases." A five-judge plurality affirmed the abortion rights granted by *Roe v. Wade*, although the facts of the case did not call for such affirmation. By a 5-to-4 margin, abortion remained a constitutional right. Despite this affirmation, the Court permitted greater retrictions on abortion by the states.)

The *Webster* decision invites state legislatures to enact abortion regulation, thus returning to the limitation that prevailed before the January 22, 1973, *Roe* decision. Justice Blackmun in a very strongly worded dissenting opinion deplored that the Webster decision "casts into darkness the hopes and visions of every woman in this country who had come to believe that the constitution guaranteed her the right to exercise some control over her unique ability to bear children." He saw also the overturn of a constitutional decision as "a rare and grave undertaking." By its decision, Justice Blackmun concluded, the plurality invited deserved "charges of cowardice and illegitimacy to our door."

As a rule, judges are supposed to adhere to continuity by affirming the decisions of their predecessors. The way the courts have interpreted the abortion laws has not been fixed and invariable due to the constantly changing political forces to which the courts react. Since the courts, especially the Supreme Court, are not insensitive to the public mood, the changes that occur in society have an impact on the courts' opinions. The judges often adapt their decisions to what Justice Holmes called "the felt necessities of the time."

How far should the adaptation go? The Attorney General during the Reagan administration, William French

Smith, remarked that when "courts fail to exercise self-restraint and instead enter the political realms reserved to the elected branches, they subject themselves to political pressure endemic to the arena and invite popular attack." (*The Wall Street Journal*, April 19, 1984, p. 30.) Among the controversies that invite such a "popular attack" is the abortion issue.

Political debate, however vigorous or even partisan, is a normal and healthy manifestation of our democratic system of government. Of no less importance for the preservation of our democracy is the nonpartisan administration of justice. There seems to be a growing tendency to appoint judges based on their political ideology rather than on their knowledge, experience, and prominence as jurists. I hope that the time will never come in this country when the courts become instruments of the party and the judicial power is subordinated to the political end of assuring the continued authority of the party in power.

Whenever, to my great regret, I hear judges described as "conservative or liberal," I am reminded of Edmund Burke's inspiring concept of justice, "There is but one law for all, namely, that law which governs all law, the law of our Creator, the law of humanity, justice, equity—the law of nature, and of nations." (*Impeachment of Warren Hastings*, 28 May 1794.) Or, as Chief Justice Hughes stated in the *Macintosh* case: "But in the form of conscience, duty to a moral power higher than the state has always been maintained." (283 U.S. 51 S. Ct. 570, 578 [1930].)

The varying philosophical views of the Justices of the Supreme Court are reflected in a long list of cases highlighted by 5-to-4 decisions. Obviously, the dissenting opinions of Justices denouncing the decisions of the majority of their fellow Justices, are prompted by conflicting moral values. History and experience yield evidence that when these values are subjected to the sanctions emanating from the opinions of society, the conflict can be reduced by a common denominator, namely, responsibility to our fellowman and to society.

Harmonizing Two Moral Perspectives

According to Professor Reinhold Niebuhr, whom we quoted above, there is a conflict between individual and social morality. The contradiction between them, he wrote, is not absolute, but "neither are they easily harmonized." We agree that there is a line of distinction between the private individual morality calling for unselfishness and the public morality with justice being its highest ideal. But there is evidence that harmony can be achieved between these two moral perspectives.

The common denominator is based on two premises. First, there is the sanctity of the individual and his duty to use his talents and abilities as a self-reliant but responsible citizen. Second, side by side with private responsibilities we should acknowledge societal and governmental responsibilities and commitment for social improvement. Man is a social being, one that cannot exist apart from the community, and the morality of the community is an aggregate of the "moral sense" of all the individuals forming the community. Both individual and social morality can be consistent with the principle of service to our fellowman. Individuals as well as society must accept sacrifices for the common good.

In each society we may find contentious groups that

selfishly protect their own interest. Despite their opposition to efforts to enable others to live in decency—opposition often expressed by a barrage of irrational assertions—the record shows that reason triumphs over emotions and that we have achieved remarkable progress.

Let us give some examples of the progress that has occurred and is still taking place. In spite of resistance to school taxes and school bond issues, the public school system is expanding. One of the spectacular phenomena of this century is the extension of educational opportunity to more and more people. There is also an undeniable shift in enrollment in institutions of higher learning to tax-supported schools. At the beginning of this century, 80 percent of all students were in private and church-related colleges and universities, and only 20 percent in tax-supported institutions. It is estimated that this figure will be reversed before the end of the century.

Until the great depression of the 1930s the economic blows caused by unemployment, sickness, accidents, occupational injury and old age remained essentially a personal responsibility. Relief provided by the government and charitable institutions was scanty and often humiliating. In 1937 the Social Security Act went into effect, and the federal relief program was undertaken on a major scale. Along with a public works program, a social security system was designed to protect the American people against the main causes of economic insecurity—unemployment, sickness, old age, and accidents. In spite of the fact that some of the citizens' groups disapproved and fought against the program, the social security system continued to grow, and its scope was extended.

Old-age survivors' insurance, unemployment insurance, public assistance to the needy, workers' compensation, provisions for the blind and children, Medicare, Medicaid, the guaranteed minimum wage, and other protective social legislation, although still far from meeting the public morality's ideal of economic justice, are characterized by a sense of social responsibility for our fellowman.

The drive for equal voting rights regardless of gender, race, and color, civil rights legislation, and legislation against discriminatory employment practices have for their purpose to redress the imbalance reflecting underrepresentation of women and minorities in political life and in the labor market. In governmental agencies and private business organizations, the employer, stated the Supreme Court in 1987, did not "trammel the rights of male employees" by promoting a woman over a male employee with a higher test score. (*Paul E. Johnson v. Transportation Agency, Santa Clara County, California, et al.*, 107 S. Ct. 1444 [1987].)

As we mentioned above, discrimination in reverse is not a solution because two wrongs do not make right, but there is no doubt that we have made enormous progress toward achieving equality. In the political arena women and minorities have made great gains in terms of the number of elected officials. The judicial system, including the Supreme Court that once upheld segregation, is now racially integrated, and there are many women now serving on the bench as well. When the dispossessed and starved Irish arrived in this country, signs reading "No Irish allowed" went up in restaurants, and others reading "We do not rent to Irish" were posted on houses. In this century, Irish names grace the rosters of high public officials—including Congressmen, Senators, and Presidents—and of every profession and calling.

In Mississippi, which once wrote a tragic chapter of assassination of civil rights leaders engaged in the struggle for integration, the state legislature now has more blacks than that of any other state in the Union. Women and members of minority groups now occupy the City Halls of some of America's largest cities. In President Bush's cabinet a woman was Secretary of Labor and a black doctor Secretary of Health and Human Services. The cabinet appointed by President Clinton emerged as the most diverse in the nation's history. It includes three women, four African-Americans, and two hispanics. Also, for the first time in the history of the United States, a black man, General Colin Powell, served as Chairman of the Joint Chiefs of Staff.

The purpose of this lecture is not to list all the accomplishments in response to the voice of national conscience. Although in our generation that voice has become louder, the reality is that there will always be a gap between the public morality's ideal of justice and what we can accomplish. The same gap will exist between the individual morality calling for unselfishness and the individual's readiness to make sacrifices. Morality's call is expressed in the assertion of Jesus in the Gospel that "anything you did for my brothers here, however humble, you did for me." (Matthew 25:40.) There will always be a time for grander goals that seem to elude the individual's or society's grasp. The goals the individual and society have been seeking for so long, however, will be closer to achievement when the individual and society share their responsibility toward their fellowman and toward society.

These goals will be closer to achievement when our traditional value structure that gives primacy to the dignity of the individual has been restored and when society's concern in guaranteeing that dignity is again stressed. Only then will our people and society remain free. Only then will we be acting in accordance with the advice St. Paul gave to a young friend: "Timothy, keep safe what has been entrusted to you." (I Timothy 6:20.)

RESPONSIBILITY AND ITS PERVERSIONS

by

Harvey C. Mansfield

Harvey C. Mansfield, Jr.

Harvey C. Mansfield, Jr., is Frank G. Thomson Professor of Government at Harvard University. He earned his A.B. in 1953 and his Ph.D. in 1961, both from Harvard, and taught at the University of California at Berkeley for two years before joining the Harvard faculty in 1962. He served as Chairman of the Department of Government from 1973 to 1977.

Professor Mansfield was awarded a Guggenheim Fellowship in 1970–71 and a National Endowment for the Humanities Fellowship in 1974–75. He was a member of the council of the American Political Science Association in 1980–82 and a fellow of the National Humanities Center in 1982. He served on the Board of Foreign Scholarships of the United States Information Agency from 1987 to 1989 and has been a member of the Advisory Council of the National Endowment for the Humanities since 1991.

In addition to many articles in journals and books, Professor Mansfield is the author of Statesmanship and Party Government, A Study of Burke and Bolingbroke *(1965),* The Spirit of Liberalism *(1978),* Machiavelli's New Modes and Orders: A Study of the Discourses on Livy *(1979),* Taming the Prince: The Ambivalence of Modern Executive Power *(1989), and* America's Constitutional Soul *(1991). His edition of* Selected Letters of Edmund Burke *appeared in 1984, and he has since published translations of* Machiavelli's The Prince *(1985) and* Machiavelli's Florentine Histories *(with Laura F. Banfield, 1988).*

RESPONSIBILITY AND ITS PERVERSIONS*

by

Harvey C. Mansfield

Before responsibility can be perverted, it has to be discovered. "Meeting our responsibilities" is a fine phrase we often use, but where do we go to meet them? When that question has been adequately answered, it will be time to consider what has happened to responsibility in our postmodern democracy. The troubles of responsibility, I shall argue, come out of the very individualism that nourishes it. Our inconspicuous bourgeois virtue called *responsibility* is most endangered by its close relatives.

I

Responsibility is an inconspicuous virtue because it does not announce itself as a virtue simply to be praised. One can be blamed as well as praised when one is held *responsible* for some fact or deed, for the word originally means "to be the cause of," whether for good or ill. Responsibility comes from a morally neutral source that suppresses or covers over the usual prideful tendency of moral virtue to boast. The moral person is often given to

*This essay relies on, and borrows from, three previous discussions of mine in Harvey C. Mansfield, *Taming the Prince*, Johns Hopkins Paperbacks, 1993, ch. 10; *America's Constitutional Soul*, Johns Hopkins Paperbacks, 1993, ch. 10; and *Old Rights and New*, Robert A. Licht, ed., AEI Press, 1993, ch. 5.

vaunting his moral virtue and contrasting it with the viciousness of others who deserve to be blamed, like Brutus complaining about Cassius in Shakespeare's *Julius Caesar*. The responsible person is more modest. He lets himself be praised and allows others to draw comparisons between his willingness to take charge and the weakness of others who hang back and allow things to happen.

Responsibility as a virtue first shows up in a political context in America. Though the word had been used before, the quality is first discussed extensively in *The Federalist*, in which, the computer says, the word occurs thirty-six times. It is said especially to describe the relationship of the Senate and the President to the people. They are responsible to the people when they are not being merely responsive to the people's desires but, more soberly, when they do what the people cannot do for themselves but will be found, in the next election or after things settle down, to approve of. Thus in its first usage responsibility is a combination of acting on one's own— "taking the initiative" or "taking charge" as Americans say—and acting on behalf of someone else, the people or society in general. In the latter aspect, the responsible official is guided ultimately, though not immediately, by what the people want and is therefore a neutral instrument.

In that context, responsibility also appears as a democratic virtue. Though the responsible person is outstanding, it is because he has been made so by the gratitude of the people. Their gratitude may be delayed, so that the responsible person must expect to wait for it, but it will come. Thus, while responsibility is elevating, it does not separate the responsible person from his fellow citizens; it is not aristocratic. It lacks the flavor of aristocracy that

Aristotle's eleven moral virtues have and that required him to consider a society that aims at virtue generally as aristocratic. Responsibility is a way of accommodating virtue without giving it pretensions. It is the *noblesse oblige* of a society that has no established nobility and does not cultivate noble disdain.

If we continue the comparison with Aristotle, we can see that responsibility replaces magnanimity, the most aristocratic virtue, the one that gathers all the other virtues and adorns them with the virtue of knowing one is virtuous. The responsible person is courageous, moderate, generous, magnificent (if he is lucky to have enough money), has the right amount of anger, tells the truth, is friendly, and is certainly just. The one virtue in which he is probably lacking is wit, for his responsibility weighs on him somewhat, keeps him earnest, and denies him the opportunity to learn to be graceful. The responsible person does not have the opportunity to learn about the world or to indulge youthful passions in pointless amusement. He is always too busy, and when young, he is full of his plans for the future (which, of course, he is always ready to set aside should his responsibility call for it). The one virtue he has above all is the right amount of ambition, since it is his ambition that replaces the magnanimity of the aristocrat. Aristotle notes that men are blamed both for too little and for too much ambition (indeed, they are still), so that there must be a right amount in between. The ambivalence of ambition, good or bad, corresponds to that of responsibility, for good as for evil. Aristotle states the premise of moral virtue as a whole that "man appears to be the first cause." What is the premise of virtue for Aristotle becomes the principal virtue for us, since we moderns believe so firmly in man

the maker of his destiny. Where he said man *appears to
be* the first cause, we say he *is*.

When man is understood as the maker of his own
destiny, each individual person must be considered distinct from his fellows. The reason is that man as maker
would in the best case owe nothing to whatever or
whoever made him; he would have no obligation to
nature or God. But this means that he would have no
obligation to other men who have been placed here by
nature or God: he accepts no inheritances and makes, or
makes over, everything for himself. Man the maker
makes over only man's individual destiny, and the glory
of mankind is necessarily expressed in the glory of
individuals who have benefitted mankind, but only as a
means of benefitting themselves. Thus the great project
of raising the status of humanity as a species that began
in the early modern period of history is necessarily
accompanied by a denial of humanity as a virtue. No-
where is this clearer than in the thought of Machiavelli,
who began the project. Machiavelli promised to work for
"the common benefit of each," meaning the benefit of
each as an individual in common with all other individuals. But to do this he also taught men how to use cruelty
well, that is, for a common benefit, and not waste it on
superfluous revenge.

All I am saying is that the modern project of man's
controlling his destiny brought with it modern individualism. The new responsibility of man entailed a new ir-
responsibility of man, because modern man is both more
and less humane than his despised predecessors. Hence
a problem arose that was resolved, or at least treated,
by the virtue of responsibility.

Machiavelli's formulation of the problem has proved

to be too sharp for our taste, although for penetrating insight it has not yet been matched. The liberal individualism that followed Machiavelli's moralized and regularized his version—thus covering it over rather than eliminating it. Liberal individualism is expresssed in two different ways that are still very much with us today: individual rights and self-interest. Rights are the formal argument of liberal individualism; interests are its informal essence. Rights were set forth in their classical formulation by John Locke, who spoke little, and disparagingly, of interests. Interests are best explained by Adam Smith, who had nothing much to say about rights. But I will treat them as parts of one system in order to set the stage for responsibility.

A right is something an individual can do, but is not required to do. He may exercise the right in company with others, for example in the right of consent to government, which he *must* exercise with others. But a right belongs to the individual to exercise at his discretion and at his initiative on his own behalf. One cannot, therefore, have a right to an impossible condition, such as immortality, as rights are about actions, not wishes. Rights are rights against the interference of other human beings, not against nature. Since a right is left to the discretion of the individual, it states a range of possible behavior, and so, as I said, it is formal. The right of free speech, for example, leaves open what will be said.

Interest, however, tells how you will exercise your right: You will use it in your interest. So interest predicts what will in fact happen in a society of rights—for example, that the right of free speech will not be abused by everyone's condemning one another because it is in no one's interest to do so. Interest, one can say, supplies the discipline of a society of rights. A society of rights is persuaded with claims and counterclaims of rights; it is full of what has aptly been called "rights talk." Self-interest works quietly through the clamor, vanity, and extravagance of rights talk and reduces it to a calculation of actual advantages. So if self-interest does not succeed in moderating free speech, it can ignore it. The right of free speech, in particular, seems designed not only to enable us to deliberate on policies and to produce works of literature and philosophy without hindrance, but also simply to let off steam. Interest allows us to keep our eye on the main chance while indulging our fancies.

But is interest sufficient to the task of supplying prudence to a society of rights? What of certain bothersome jobs that need to be done but are not very rewarding, at least in terms that can be calculated? One thinks immediately of what used to be called "women's work," the work that is never done (meaning, finished), that is still in fact done mostly by women. Besides jobs of drudgery there are also, on the contrary, jobs of risk—including the holding of high office in politics or business—which might easily appear to be against one's interest to perform. The counsel of interest might well be "let George do it." This is known in political economy today as the free rider problem. It seems to be in your interest not to volunteer to serve a common interest, such as household work or high office, when you can hope someone else will be sucker enough to do it. When we move from individual or particular interest to common interests, even when the common interests are shared more or less equally by individuals (for example, protection from crime), self-interest seems to falter.

Here is where responsibility enters. Responsibility

can be defined as taking charge in a situation of risk or drudgery in order to improve it, a situation from which others shrink because they think that inaction is in their interest. It is a duty or virtue, but only in *our* sense, in the context of a society that believes in rights and practices its interests. In the usual, traditional sense (still alive today among the religious and the soldierly), duty implies devotion to something higher than oneself; and virtue implies a concern with the perfection of one's soul. But our society of rights seems to say that human beings are sovereign, and indeed rights were first conceived in the seventeenth century in order to reject claims of divine right and to suppress the interference of priests in government. Virtue, too, as we have seen, seems aristocratic; in calling for perfection, virtue seems confined to a few whom the rest of us should admire and perhaps obey. Responsibility, however, is exercised in the more democratic context of rights and interests, which are the two beacons of our moral and political life. Rights are wider than one's responsibility since the range of behavior under a right includes irresponsible actions. And interests are narrower, because one's interest is often to avoid the risk of a responsible action.

Yet if responsibility is not identical to rights and interests, it is not antithetical to them either. A right includes, although it does not require, responsible action. So a responsible person can claim that he has a right to act responsibly if he has a right to act at all, and the fact that he is not required to act underlines the voluntary character, and the merit, of his action. Responsibility, like virtue but unlike duty, is self-assumed. And because the responsible person has a right to his responsibility, the irresponsible cannot so easily get in his way.

Nor is it so clear, on second thought, that responsibility is inconsistent with self-interest. Although one's interest may counsel abstractly against exposing oneself to risk, one's concrete interest may be attached to a position in which he is made responsible for certain actions. Responsibility usually goes with a job, and enough people will believe that reputation or fame for having done the job well is in their interest.

Thus responsibility is linked to interest even if it is not the same. We are reminded of the phrase "the interest of the office," which occurs in *The Federalist*. Publius (author of that work) argued that the interest of the office would encourage responsible behavior in the officers of the American Constitution. It is noteworthy that our notion of responsibility does not occur in the thought of John Locke, the founder of liberalism, who speaks ambiguously of duties to God, to mankind, or to one's interest. Our notion seems to begin in *The Federalist*, in which one sees liberalism no longer merely in theory but at work in the framing of a new constitution. Liberalism at work is in need of responsibility; rights and interests are both too theoretical to suffice by themselves. Rights are too formal; they merely state a range of possible actions, some good, some bad, that may or may not be followed, and with greatness, mediocrity, or ruin as the outcome. Interests are too mechanical and too much on the average. A society that follows its interest may avoid the depths of degradation but will never achieve greatness. Its mediocrity will make liberty seem unattractive and may give opportunity to movements such as communism and fascism that are nourished by boring bourgeois mediocrity and that rebel against the lack of challenge in following one's interest. Responsibility is the answer to the contingency of rights and the all-too-evident predictability of interest. In a liberal society many people have to be willing to take actions for which, in rights theory and in systems of self-interest, they may lack sufficient reason. Responsibility is the free way to solve the problems of a free society. Rights offer too much freedom, interests too little. Responsibility offers what a right cannot specify and what your interest cannot quite ensure.

The responsible person is restless, always on the move, searching for an opportunity. In this he typifies the ever-watchfulness of self-interest. He is in *pursuit* of happiness, and he will probably never get there. His satisfactions do not supply the sense of rest in Aristotle's notion of perfect and complete happiness. There is always something more to do. For the responsible person does things; he gets results. Others sit around and wish that someone would do something; he gets up and does what needs to be done. Good intentions are not enough for responsibility; the responsible person must have skills and abilities, and must cultivate them. He improves himself more by acting than by taking courses in a university. He knows what he can and cannot do.

The responsible person's desire to produce results does not lead him into Machiavellian criminality, in which the good result excuses the evil means used to get it. He might well feel obliged to read Machiavelli so as to acquaint himself with the range of tests and temptations that the world can offer and also to learn just how far ambition can go. But he would disagree with Machiavelli that ordinary people are most impressed by sensational deeds which put them in fear of their governors. He might think that their loyalty can be secured by steady performance and competent action in emergencies. After experience of responsible government, the hearts of citizens will be won over; they will become attached to their government and not merely fearful. Thus the demand for results, which first appears in modern thought in Machiavelli's clarion call for *veritá effettuale* (going to the "effectual truth" of things), can be elevated to a requirement of good performance that avoids depending on astonishing acts of criminality. The responsible person, like the Machiavellian prince, must do the job and be seen to have done it; but unlike that prince, he does not rely on fear, and the means he uses can bear public examination.

The Federalist makes a particular point of responsibility in the executive. The new American presidency, it claims, will be more responsible because it is an office for one man who will be accountable rather than for a committee whose members have no individual responsibility. The President will, because of the lengthy tenure of his office, have "personal firmness"; he will not be tempted into a "servile pliancy" to the Congress, to other governments, or to the people. With such an office there is "due dependence" on the people as befits republican government, but there is also due responsibility: The President, while remaining dependent, is elevated out of the vices of servility and overcaution that usually go with dependence. The President will combine energy with republican safety. *Energy* is another very American word linked to responsibility by *The Federalist*, and discussed there for the first time. The responsible person is full of energy; he is restless, but his motions are well controlled. He is not at all averse to risk, for in the famous phrase, "love of fame is the ruling passion of the noblest minds." The noblest minds are animated by self-interest, but it is *their* self-interest, that of the noblest minds. Responsibility is not confined to the American presidency, but it has its origins in *The Federalist*'s description of the office, elaborated from the bare formal terms given in the Constitution. Responsibility is America's constitutional virtue, the virtue taught by our Constitution and required for its operation not only in the specific constitutional offices but more widely in all jobs public and private.

Another connection between responsibility and self-interest is in private property. Although you can follow your interest universally, under any economic system, the system most in your interest is the one that allows you to pursue it freely, which is capitalism. Capitalism is the economic system that provides the most opportunity for restless motion, so that individuals are constantly on the lookout for new attachments and expanded interests. A statist system, on the contrary, confines the pursuit of interest to bureaucratic maneuvering for the impairment or exclusion of others' interests. It discourages individual responsibility because one's interest is always to make the government assume responsibility for the maneuvers so as to conceal them. But when you can own the company, it is in your interest to start it, and thereby take responsibility for it. The entrepreneurial spirit consists of the desire to make money, the desire to do so by making something new, the desire to be a success, the desire to be seen as a success, and the desire to do what makes one be seen as a success. Here is a progression by easy stages from self-interest to responsibility, which is made possible only through the many opportunities characteristic of a society of private property. George Gilder had the right idea but the wrong name when he spoke of the *altruism* of capitalists. Their virtue is precisely not altruism, which is opposed to self-interest but rather responsibility, which grows out of self-interest.

Responsibility is, then, the answer to the problem of the free rider, the person who believes that his interest lies in letting someone else take the responsibility. The free rider has to suppress his pride when declining responsibility, as he admits when he says complacently, "Let someone else take the glory," implying that glory is nothing but trouble. Now, it is true that in the first place interest is opposed to pride. One's interest is never to make an issue of oneself and get angry, because one might thereby pass up a profitable transaction with a disagreeable person. But on reflection, the ability to stay cool in such situations is a sign of a self-mastery in which one can take legitimate pride. We could even say that all of one's other interests depend on the development of a calm, collected self. Responsibility, then, is nourished by pride and/or interest in having the kind of self, or being the sort of person, who is useful in situations in which someone must take charge. And of course, being a responsible sort of person is not clear either to others or to oneself without a demonstration. To justify his pride, the responsible person must get us the results we all expect from him. Perhaps the free rider's inaction will be in his interest if he has something better to do with his time than act responsibly, some higher, contemplative pursuit. But if not, his self-congratulation at having done the clever thing is apt, and even likely, to fade as he begins to wonder whether he was *capable* of a responsible action.

Although most responsibilities go with jobs, the situation in which someone must take charge reminds us that the highest responsibility is to act precisely when it is no one's job or responsibility. The American presidency, the office from which I believe we originally get our notion of responsibility, is concerned with aspects of politics that go beyond the routine and are full of risk; these are long-term enterprises and their opposite, quick strokes in dangerous emergencies. The President's job, if it can be called that, is to do what is no one else's job. Others who act responsibly beyond the requirements of their jobs imitate the requirements of his. It seems that maintaining control of events demands a healthy recognition that a network of offices with a table of organization is not enough; unpredictable circumstances will present themselves, and someone will have to step out of the confines of his usual post to take the responsibility for going beyond his responsibilities. In the American language this is known as *initiative*.

We have now arrived at a paradox: The highest responsibility is accepting responsibility for things one has not been responsible for. A responsible person is someone who takes charge precisely in a difficult situation he did not cause—for which he was not responsible. And if someone chooses to do something foolish, we call him *responsible* for that action; but we also consider him *irresponsible* for choosing to do something foolish. That paradox of language arises from a difficulty in the fact of responsibility. To take charge of a situation means to take control of a situation previously uncontrolled. But how can we suppose ourselves capable of controlling everything, as if we were gods? Of course we cannot, but in making the choices in our actions or policies, we must take account of things that necessarily accompany our choices. To take an example from Thomas Aquinas: If you choose to walk in the hot sun, you choose to perspire.

In one sense, you did not choose to perspire, but since it is a necessity of our nature that cannot be wished away to perspire in the hot sun, in another sense you chose to perspire as a known consequence of walking in the hot sun. When you choose to do something, you assume responsibility for everything in that situation which you did not choose or would not have chosen. You assume responsibility for all the regularities of *nature*, including those you were not aware of but could have known, and all the irregularities of nature too, known as *chance*, since it is perfectly knowable that not everything is knowable. The responsible person makes himself the representative of nature or God, accepting the situation in which he takes responsibility as his own. This means that he takes responsibility for the whole of that situation, which, when you think about it, is, simply, all nature and all chance.

At the same time, however, the responsibile person knows that he is *not* God, that he cannot choose everything. The responsible person "knows what he is doing" in a double sense: He knows what to do, and he is aware of his limitations. Irresponsible people are not only those who do not know what to do but also those who want everything their own way and will not accept what they do not like. The first sort are fools, who are somehow less irresponsible than the second sort, who are willful. The responsible person knows both his limitations and the constraints in the situation, and he accepts them.

II

With this conclusion, we have come some distance from our beginning, where responsibility was seen to depend on the modern thought that man is the maker of his own destiny. That idea is not truly consistent with recognition of the limitations on responsibility that we have just discussed. Indeed, the virtue of responsibility is much more heavily laden with theory than Aristotle's moral virtues, which were deliberately isolated by Aristotle from contamination by theory. As noted above, responsibility was for him the principle of moral virtue rather than a virtue. Individualism, the central idea of modernity, has created both the need and the opportunity for responsibility—the need, because individualism is self-interested and thus likely to be selfish; the opportunity, because duty and virtue, the alternatives to responsibility, are disfavored. The development of modern thought has, however, created three enemies of responsibility, three modes of theorizing that attack or undermine it. They are passivity, selflessness, and self-expression. I shall describe them briefly and illustrate them from Hobbes, Kant, and Nietzsche.

The danger of passivity comes from modern science, both natural and political. The fundamental notion of modern science has two aspects. First, science was expected to extend human power over nature. Nature does not have to be accepted as it is; it is neither our friend nor our master. Nature can be subdued and made to serve human needs. But, in the second place, science will narrow human responsibility so that we are responsible only for what we make. We must learn to distinguish between what is imposed on us—nature and chance—and what we make artificially, to serve our needs.

But what results from the distinction between what is imposed on us and what we make? It seems that from the rejection of things as they are and have been we can greatly extend our responsibility. Instead of accepting nature's species, for example, we can improve them with hybrids. There is a drawback, however. Once we have learned how to make something, we cannot turn back and forget how to make it. We become as much prisoners of our artifices as we used to be of nature's limitations, and the extent of our responsibility seems to have diminished rather than increased.

An obvious example is television. Television gives us a new power to see things at a distance, but once we begin to watch it, we lose our capacity to concentrate on things around us. We seem to know more about Bosnia and Somalia than about our neighborhoods. But do we really know what we see on television? "Television" in German is *Fernsehen*, far seeing; would anyone say that because of television our generation is more far-seeing than previous ones? Television seems to remove us from the everyday things around us, on which we can act, and to send us to far-off events about which we can only feel, or sympathize. And thinking it over, we realize that we did not really invent television; someone invented it for us, and we had no choice or responsibility. Technology seems in general to have become our master, rather than remaining our servant. We have become passive rather than responsible citizens.

One can see the same consequences in modern political science, which comes from Hobbes. According to modern political science, men can make their government from the ground up. Aristotle had said that man by nature is a political animal, so that our responsibility is not to choose whether to have government, but which kind. Hobbes greatly expanded our responsibility by denying that we have to accept our political nature. Instead, we can imagine ourselves in a nonpolitical state of nature in which we can decide whether to have government at all, not merely which kind. But the expanded responsibility is a delusion. Life in the state of nature is so unbearable that we find ourselves compelled of necessity to create the government (by a social contract) for which we allegedly had no natural inclination. Again, we have to accept what we began by supposing we could make, and after attempting to widen our responsibility, we are stuck with less of it. For if we must passively submit to the necessity of government even as we make it, it is hard to see how we can recover our capacity to be responsible afterwards. When we try to make everything from the ground up, we fall into accepting everything that has been made. The citizen who tries to create government ends up submitting to it, like the grumbling nonvoters of our day who say they want to overthrow the whole system and actually do nothing. With citizenship as with technology, too much responsibility becomes too little.

Two attempts to cure the problem of passivity have made it worse. The first of these, associated with Kant, was to try to find a secure place for moral freedom and thus for moral responsibility. Hobbes's system had left man, the maker of his own destiny, immersed in the necessities to which he must conform in his making; and so those necessities mastered him. The necessity of technology, the necessity of government that inspire his invention somehow take over his life, and what begins as an instrument for overcoming necessities turns out merely to create new ones. But it is one's self-interest that causes one to submit to these necessities. Perhaps one could transcend self-interest by positing the possibility that each individual could make moral judgments, not on the basis of his circumstances or of the circumstances of his friends or fellow citizens, but by legislating for all rational beings. Then your self-interest, by being universalized, is transformed into selflessness, and your responsibility is magnified to an awesome degree. Instead of merely running your own life, you become a legislator for all rational beings and take responsibility for legislating all morality, again from the ground up. You can do this because, by the very act of legislating universally, you have lifted yourself above the necessities which apply to you when you think of your interests, your attachments.

Yet again, this noble and extremely influential scheme is inimical to the responsibility that is practicable for us. One can transcend the circumstances of our lives, and issue absolute moral commands valid for all rational beings, only by ignoring the consequences of various moral judgments. Thus the test of morality comes to be, not whether it will improve the situation in which it is applied, but whether the intent of the moral person (legislating for all rational beings) was good. Morality descends to moralism when it refuses to look at consequences. The moral person preens himself on his purity rather than taking charge of a situation in which others with whom he must deal are not so well intentioned. He thinks that he is above them, and freer than they because they are caught in selfish interests, but the truth is just to the contrary. His conscientiousness is constrained, not empowered, by his morality, and such a person is less free to act responsibly. He rejects limited reforms unless he can change the world, and his assumption of God's responsibility—to make the moral law—

renders him irresponsible in the affairs of men.

Besides, it proves impossible to ignore the realm of necessity in which our interests lie. This was the case for Kant, and it is the same for his many followers today. Kant tried to show that historical conditions, though strictly separate from morality, were nevertheless developing so that moral actions were becoming more profitable. Today, his argument appears in the widespread concern for the *root causes* of our ills. Root causes such as poverty or patriarchy or violence on television admittedly do not cause particular individuals to misbehave; but it is thought that by attacking those causes we will improve the environment of morality and morality itself will triumph because it is unimpeded. The root causes argument presupposes, contrary to the possibility of legislating for all rational beings, that people are mercenary and power-seeking; and it is hard to see how their responsibility will be improved if one never appeals to it. I conclude that it is a mistake to disconnect responsibility from self-interest. I do not claim to have refuted Kant, but perhaps with these objections—to be sure, familiar ones—I have stirred a doubt.

A second attack on the idea of self-interest has created a third enemy of the virtue of responsibility. This is the notion of self-expression that comes from Nietzsche and the postmoderns. These thinkers take the opposite course. While condemning any attempt at selflessness as ridiculous and inhuman, they become preoccupied with the self. The self, they say, does not exist prior to our concern with it; there is no fixed human nature to speak of, hence no fixed self. The self must be created, and it is created by expressing itself. *Identity* is something we must all obtain through self-expression. Thus each individual is held responsible for finding or creating his own identity: Don't expect any help from God or nature.

But here again a strange reversal occurs. The new self, lacking any natural definition, is obliged to define itself through its self-expression. It is capable of this, however, only to the extent of its energy. Those selves who are content with a conventional definition—or are too weak to oppose it—will allow themselves to be defined passively and inauthentically. The very few truly creative ones will lead them not by asking their opinion but by pushing them aside. Thus the self-expression that creates self-esteem will in fact, for the great majority apart from the few creative individuals, rest on public esteem. Taking responsibility for creating one's self reduces once again to ceding responsibility to someone else—to the public that establishes the ruling conventions.

An example of this progression is the women's movement, which has sponsored a great redefinition of the public self of women. Heretofore women have been largely excluded from "responsible positions"—those jobs from which one gains public reputation. But they took quiet satisfaction and pride instead from doing family tasks that are usually taken for granted. They took responsibility for the jobs that responsible people overlook because they have no risk and gain no reputation. These are private and nonpolitical responsibilities. Now women may still feel drawn to such jobs, at least some of the time, but because their identities must be created by public esteem, they have no justification for doing what they very well see still needs doing. Their flashy new identities do not clean the house, put supper on the table, or raise the children. Clearly, we shall not be returning any time soon, if ever, to the old dispensation that declared a woman's place to be in the home. But in the meantime we suffer from the lack of responsibility in its private aspect, now that human beings of both sexes want to be someone important. In its private aspect, responsibility means to be the cause of useful results, but not for the sake of recognition. Here responsibility is closer to the self-interest that is opposed to ambition.

The idea of man the maker is our idea. That it takes several forms is a sign of vitality, an indication that, despite its difficulties, it will not soon go away. As we seem to have discerned without much instruction from professors, responsibility is perhaps the best way to live with it. But the difficulties in that idea suggest the need for vigilance in defending responsibility from its enemies, who are indeed nothing but its perversions.

BUILDING THE CULTURE OF FREEDOM: CATHOLIC SOCIAL THOUGHT AND THE AMERICAN EXPERIMENT

by

George Weigel

George Weigel

George Weigel, the President of the Ethics and Public Policy Center, is a Roman Catholic theologian and one of America's leading commentators on issues of religion and public life.

A native of Baltimore, he was educated at St. Mary's Seminary and University in his native city and at the University of St. Michael's College in Toronto. In 1975, Mr. Weigel moved to Seattle where he was Assistant Professor of Theology and Assistant (later Acting) Dean of Studies at the St. Thomas Seminary School of Theology in Kenmore. In 1977, Mr. Weigel became Scholar-in-Residence at the World Without War Council of Greater Seattle, a position he held until 1984.

In 1984–85, Mr.Weigel was a Fellow of the Woodrow Wilson International Center for Scholars in Washington, D.C. There, he wrote Tranquillitas Ordinis: The Present Failure and Future Promise of American Catholic Thought on War and Peace. *Mr. Weigel is the author or editor of twelve other books, including* Catholicism and the Renewal of American Democracy *(1989),* Freedom and Its Discontents *(1991),* Just War and the Gulf War *(1991), and* The Final Revolution: The Resistance Church and the Collapse of Communism *(1992). In addition to his books, Mr. Weigel has contributed op-ed columns, essays, and reviews to most of the major opinion journals and newspapers in the United States.*

From 1986 until 1989, Mr. Weigel served as Founding President of the James Madison Foundation. In 1989, he assumed his present position at the Ethics and Public Policy Center. There he has led a wide-ranging ecumenical and inter-religious program of research and publication on foreign and domestic policy issues.

Mr. Weigel serves on the boards of directors of several organizations dedicated to human rights and the cause of religious freedom. He is also a member of the editorial boards of First Things, The Washington Quarterly, *and* Orbis.

BUILDING THE CULTURE OF FREEDOM: CATHOLIC SOCIAL THOUGHT AND THE AMERICAN EXPERIMENT

by

George Weigel

Adam's legendary comment to Eve on their way out of the Garden of Eden—"We live, my dear, in a time of transition"—has rarely been so frequently invoked as in the three years just past; the years since the collapse of European communism marked the end of the Fifty-Five Years' War against totalitarianism. Yet that mantra, "a time of transition," has usually been understood as referring to something "out there"—the assumption being that we in the West have achieved the "end of history" in our consolidation of liberal democratic polities and market economies. On this understanding of our situation, most brilliantly and provocatively argued by Francis Fukuyama, all that remains for us is the fine-tuning of western political and economic systems in order to solve "technical problems," assuage "environmental concerns," and satisfy "sophisticated consumer demands." (Francis Fukuyama, "The End of History?" *The National Interest* 16, Summer 1989, p. 16.)

But just as the collapse of communism has not meant the "end of history" in Central and Eastern Europe but rather the return of history to its normal patterns and rhythms, so the victory of the West in the Fifty-Five Years' War has not seen the inauguration of the kingdom of righteousness, truth, and justice here among us. Indeed, in one of those ironies that frequently mark the turnings of history, the crisis of communism may be followed in short order by the crisis of liberal democracy or democratic capitalism. Moreover, and to illustrate the venerable axiom that there are many ironies in the fire, the crisis of liberal democracy will be similar to the crisis of communism in one crucial respect: Were it to descend upon us with full fury, the crisis of the West will be an "anthropological" crisis, in which a false idea of the human person and human community leads to tremendous stress, and ultimately to breakdown, within our political and economic systems—precisely as did communism's "anthropological" errors.

Communism failed for many reasons: It was economically inefficient, technologically backward, culturally stultifying, politically cruel. But above all, communism failed because communism was a heresy: a congeries of false teachings about the nature of man, about human community, human history, and human destiny. Those false teachings provided the ideological rationale for the political and economic institutions that communist societies created. And the failures of those institutions—in governance, production, distribution, and consumption—were adumbrated in the errors of communism as a doctrine.

(A brief interpolation: I do not mean to argue here, in a fashion familiar to both the unrepentant left and the isolationist/libertarian right, that since communism would likely have failed anyway, containment—and its revivification by Ronald Reagan, Margaret Thatcher, and Helmut Kohl—was unnecessary and wasteful. The grave "anthropological" errors of communism would ultimately have led to the failure of the communist experiment in social engineering. But absent containment, the immense human suffering that communism caused would have been extended even farther, and the demise of the communist system would have been delayed long into the future. Communism collapsed when it did, and how it did, because of a combination of western foreign and military policies, on the one hand, and a moral-cultural revolution that made possible the re-creation of civil society in Central and Eastern Europe, on the other.)

Similarly, the crisis of liberal democratic society that may soon be upon us (if, indeed, we are not already embroiled in it) has an "anthropological" root in a great debate over the nature of man. That debate is publicly focused, in the United States, on the meaning of human freedom. And on this question, a culture war of potentially explosive consequence has broken out.

The American Culture War

In one corner, we have those who would agree with Professor Rocco Buttiglione (a careful and sympathetic student of the American scene, a distinguished Italian philosopher, and an adviser to Pope John Paul II) that "Nothing good can be done without freedom, but freedom is not the highest value in itself. Freedom is given to man in order to make possible the free obedience to truth and the free gift of oneself in love." This understanding of freedom and its relationship to the nature of the human person yields a concept of democracy as a substantive moral experiment: Democratic self-governance is never finally secured, and each generation must answer the question as to whether "a nation so conceived and so dedicated can long endure."

In the other corner are those who argue that freedom is

constituted by the liberty to pursue one's personal gratifications as one defines those gratifications, so long as no
one else (or at least no one else in whom the state asserts a
"compelling interest") gets hurt. This sensibility is not
only encountered in the academic fever swamps where
tenured radicals celebrate the joys of debonair nihilism;
in fact, this anorexic concept of freedom was succinctly
formulated in June 1992 by Supreme Court Justices
Anthony Kennedy, Sandra Day O'Connor, and David
Souter in their joint opinion in the case of *Casey v.
Planned Parenthood of S.E. Pennsylvania*: "At the heart
of liberty is the right to define one's own concept of
existence, of meaning, of the universe, and of the
mystery of human life." (112 S.Ct. 2791, 2807.) On this
understanding of things, democracy is merely an ensemble of procedures, largely legal, by which we regulate the pursuit of personal satisfaction. There is no
substantive moral core to democracy; there is no civil
society, no community of republican virtue, no public
moral conversation, sustaining democracy; there are
only the Rules of the Game. The unencumbered, self-
constituting (some might say, imperial) Self is the *telos*
toward which the American democratic experiment is
ordered.

Those of us who have been writing about an American
Kulturkampf (or "culture war") in recent years have
sometimes been accused of exaggeration, even by colleagues sympathetic to our views on specific issues. But
with *Casey*, the culture war has been defined with un-
mistakable clarity, and its gravity has been underscored
beyond anything that any sound-bite publicist could
have proposed.

For the "center" of the U.S. Supreme Court—in a decision celebrated by the prestige press, the elite culture, most of the academy, and not a few religious leaders— has declared that republican virtue, understood as a broad communal consensus on the moral coordinates of our common life, is no part of either the inner constitution or the public architecture of "freedom" in America. Why? Because to define such a consensus and to embody it in law would, according to Kennedy, O'Connor, and Souter, be an act of "compulsion" that would deny citizens the "attributes of personhood." (*Ibid.*) And yet there are tens of millions of Americans who, with the Founders and Framers, believe precisely the opposite—who believe that rights and laws ought to be grounded in prior understandings of rights and wrongs (the alternative being governance through sheer coercion); who believe that familial and public responsibility have a higher moral status in a civilized conscience than private satisfaction; who believe, and live, as if the common good were a nobler horizon against which to conduct one's life than the narrow infinity described by the pursuit of the self-actualized, self-constituting self.

(The concept of a "narrow infinity" is a variant on G.B. Chesterton, who described the "madman" in these terms: "His mind moves in a perfect but narrow circle. A small circle is quite as infinite as a large circle; but, though it is quite as infinite, it is not so large.... There is such a thing as a narrow universality; there is such a thing as a small and cramped eternity; you may see it in many modern religions." [*Orthodoxy*, New York: Doubleday Image Books, 1959, p. 20.] Including, I might add, the religion that worships the self-constituting Imperial Self.)

These battle lines in the American *Kulturkampf* are,

admittedly, broadly described. And, if we are honest with ourselves, we might concede that the trenches in the war occasionally run through our own hearts, as well as between ourselves and others. But that there is a culture war in America today, and that the resolution of that war will determine the future of the American democratic experiment, we need not doubt. The power of ideas in history, for good and for ill, has been decisively demonstrated by the course of events in the twentieth century. How we *conceive* freedom will have much to do with the ways in which we construct and operate the political and economic *institutions* through which our freedom is mediated and publicly expressed. The possibility that those institutions could so decay that the result is social chaos, and ultimately oppression, has been recognized by wise Americans since colonial days. Whether that chaos unfolds in our time is the outcome being contested in the American *Kulturkampf*, and in the crisis of liberal democratic society that has ironically followed fast on the heels of the collapse of communism.

John Paul II on Human Freedom

In May 1991, Pope John Paul II issued *Centesimus Annus*, a social encyclical that quickly established itself as a landmark event in contemporary religious thought about human freedom and its embodiment in culture, economics, and politics. Issued to honor the centenary of Pope Leo XIII's pioneering encyclical, *Rerum Novarum*, *Centesimus Annus* ("The Hundredth Year") offers both a look back at the *res novae*, the "new things" that seized the attention of Leo XIII, and a look ahead at what we might call the "new new things," the new facts of public life, at the end of the twentieth century and the turn of the third Christian millennium. Like other papal documents, *Centesimus Annus* reaffirms the classic themes of Catholic social thought. But it is John Paul II's creative extension of the tradition that makes *Centesimus Annus* a singularly bold, and singularly relevant, document—one that reconfigures the boundaries of the Catholic debate over the right ordering of culture, economics, and politics under the conditions of modernity, and one that provides a badly needed framework for the debate over the future of ordered liberty in these United States.

Centesimus Annus is not, however, or should not be, a matter of interest to Catholics only. The encyclical addresses itself to "all men and women of good will"— which is to say, Pope John Paul II understands himself to be making *public* moral arguments, in which he invites others to engage. Moreover, and as if to prove the point, scholars, religious leaders, and politicians outside the formal boundaries of Roman Catholicism have been showing, in recent years, an increasing interest in modern Catholic social teaching as perhaps the most well-developed and coherent set of Christian reference points for conducting the argument about how Americans should order their lives, loves, and loyalties in society today. (Curiously enough, John Paul II has sometimes been more appreciated as a witness to Christian orthodoxy outside his church than within it. As a prominent Southern Baptist once put it to a group of Catholic colleagues, "Down where I come from, people are saying, 'You folks finally got yourself a pope who knows how to pope.'")

Indeed, and for the reasons suggested above, *Centesi-*

mus Annus should be of particular and urgent interest to citizens of the United States. As a nation "conceived in liberty," as the leader of the party of freedom in world politics, and as a country involved in a grave public debate over the very meaning of freedom, the United States might well pay careful attention to what the most influential moral leader in the contemporary world has to say about the many dimensions of freedom, and about the intimate relationship between freedom and truth, particularly the "truth about man" that has been such a prominent theme in the teaching of John Paul II.

Speaking in Miami in September 1987, the pope described the United States in these terms:

> "Among the many admirable values of this nation there is one that stands out in particular. It is freedom. The concept of freedom is part of the very fabric of this nation as a political community of free people. Freedom is a great gift, a great blessing of God.
>
> "From the beginning of America, freedom was directed to forming a well-ordered society and to promoting its peaceful life. Freedom was channeled to the fullness of human life, to the preservation of human dignity, and to the safeguarding of all human rights. An experience of ordered freedom is truly a part of the cherished story of this land.
>
> "This is the freedom that America is called to live and guard and to transmit. She is called to exercise it in such a way that it will also benefit the cause of freedom in other nations and among other peoples. The only true freedom, the only freedom

that can truly satisfy, is the freedom to do what we ought as human beings created by God according to his plan. It is the freedom to live the truth of what we are and who we are before God, the truth of our identity as children of God, as brothers and sisters in a common humanity. That is why Jesus Christ linked truth and freedom together, stating solemnly, 'You will know the truth and the truth will set you free' (John 8:32). All people are called to recognize the liberating truth of the sovereignty of God over them as individuals and as nations."

What John Paul II means by "freedom," of course, is not precisely what America's cultural elites have had in mind since the fevered "liberations" of the 1960s. And so an argument is upon us: What is this freedom that is a "great gift, a great blessing of God"? How is it to be lived by free men and women, in free societies that must protect individual liberty while concurrently advancing the common good?

Here, of course, the pope's concerns directly intersect the most basic issues in the American *Kulturkampf.* Thus a review of the teaching of *Centesimus Annus* may provide a moral-philosophical template for measuring the depth and breadth of our national debate over rights, responsibilities, and republican virtue.

A. The "Truth About Man" and the "Problem" of Freedom

Viewed most comprehensively, *Centesimus Annus* is a profound meditation on human nature, on man's quest for a freedom that will truly satisfy the deepest yearnings of the human heart. John Paul II does not regard

that human search for true freedom as something aber-
rant. Quite the contrary: The quest for freedom is "built
in" to the very nature of man's way of being in the world,
and "built in" precisely by a God whom we are to find,
and worship, in freedom.

Centesimus Annus (*CA*) begins with a review of the
teaching of Leo XIII in *Rerum Novarum*. For there, in
1891, the Church began to grapple with the new problem
of freedom that had been created by the upheavals of the
Industrial Revolution (in economics) and the French
Revolution (in politics). "Traditional society was passing
away and another was beginning to be formed—one
which brought the hope of new freedoms but also the
threat of new forms of injustice and servitude." (*CA*, #4.)
That threat was particularly grave when modernity ignored "the essential bond between human freedom and
truth." (*Ibid.*) Leo XIII understood, his successor argues,
that a "freedom which refused to be bound to the truth
would fall into arbitrariness and end up submitting
itself to the vilest of passions, to the point of self-destruc-
tion." (*Ibid.*) In the last decade of this bloodiest of centuries, it is difficult to suggest that Leo XIII was pre-
maturely pessimistic about certain aspects of the
modern quest for freedom.

From Leo XIII on, Catholic social teaching's "answer"
to the "problem" of freedom has begun with a moral reflection on man himself, and with an insistence on the
dignity and worth of each individual human being as a
creature endowed with intelligence and will and thus
made "in the image and likeness of God." Therefore the
beginning of the answer to the rapaciousness of Man-
chesterian liberalism in economics was "the dignity of
the worker . . . [and] the dignity of work." (*CA*, #6.) And

the beginning of the answer to the massive repression and injustice of twentieth-century tyrannies was Leo XIII's insistence on the "necessary limits to the State's intervention" in human affairs. (*CA*, #8.) Why are those limits "necessary"? Because "the individual, the family, and society are prior to the State, and . . . the State exists in order to protect their rights and not stifle them." (*CA*, #11.)

The Catholic human-rights revolution of the late twentieth century owes a large debt of gratitude to the last pope of the nineteenth century, Leo XIII. It was Leo who first pointed toward Christian *personalism* as the alternative to socialist collectivism (which subsumed human personality into the mass) and to radical individualism (which locked human personality into a self-made prison of solipsism). John Paul II, from the moment he took office in October 1978, has been a vigorous proponent of basic human rights, particularly the fundamental right of religious freedom. This pattern continues in *Centesimus Annus* in which the pope decries the situation in those countries "which covertly, or even openly, deny to citizens of faiths other than that of the majority the full exercise of their civil and religious rights, preventing them from taking part in the cultural process, and restricting both the Church's right to preach the Gospel and the right of those who hear this preaching to accept it." (*CA*, #29.)

B. Deepening the "Rights" Debate

For that reason, it is all the more striking that the human-rights language is a bit more muted in *Centesimus Annus* than in John Paul's earlier encyclicals—and far more muted than it was in Pope John XXIII's famous 1963 letter, *Pacem in Terris*. John Paul II had not suddenly become less interested in the problems of human rights. Rather, he seemed determined to deepen (and, in some respects, to discipline) the debate over "rights" by linking rights to *obligations* and to *truth*.

On this latter point, John Paul argues forcefully that conscience is not some kind of moral free agent, in which an "autonomous self" declares something to be right because it is right "for me." No, conscience is "bound to the truth." (*Ibid.*) And the truth about man is not to be confused with "an appeal to the appetites and inclinations toward immediate gratification," an appeal that is "utilitarian" in character and does not reflect "the hierarchy of the true values of human existence." (*Ibid.*)

Nor are "rights" simply a matter of our immunities from the coercive power of others (important as such immunities are). Rights exist so that we can fulfill our obligations. Thus a man should be free economically so that he can enter into more cooperative relationships with others and meet his obligations to work in order to "provide for the needs of his family, his community, his nation, and ultimately all humanity." (*CA*, #43.) Ownership, too, has its obligations: "Just as the person fully realizes himself in the free gift of self, so too ownership morally satisfies itself in the creation, at the proper time and in the proper way, of opportunities for work and human growth for all." (*Ibid.*)

By hearkening back to the Christian personalism of Leo XIII, while at the same time "thickening" the concept of "rights" in the Catholic tradition, John Paul II, in *Centesimus Annus*, provides a powerful example of Christian anthropology at its finest. But this is no abstract philosophical exercise. For having set the proper framework for thinking about public life, the pope immediately brings his analysis of the "truth about man" to bear on one of the most stunning events in this century of the unexpected—the Revolution of 1989 in Central and Eastern Europe.

C. *Revolution of the Spirit*

"The fundamental error of socialism is anthropological in nature. Socialism considers the individual person simply as an element, a molecule within the social organism, so that the good of the individual is completely subordinated to the functioning of the socio-economic mechanism. Socialism likewise maintains that the good of the individual can be realized without reference to his free choice, to the unique and exclusive responsibility he exercises in the face of good or evil. Man is thus reduced to a series of social relationships, and the concept of the person as the . . . subject of moral decision disappears, the very subject whose decisions build the social order.

"From this mistaken conception of the person there arise both a distortion of law . . . and an opposition to private property. A person who is deprived of something he can call 'his own,' and of the possibility of earning a living through his own initiative, comes to depend on the social machine and on those who control it. This makes it much more difficult for him to recognize his dignity as a person, and hinders progress toward the building up of an authentic human community." (*CA* #13.)

Western political scientists and international-relations specialists have had a hard time figuring out what happened in Central and Eastern Europe in 1989. "Delayed modernization" seems to be the preferred answer; the economic systems of the Communist world could not compete, and the only way to change them was to get rid of the political regimes that had imposed collectivism in the first place. It is, in truth, a deliciously (if depressingly) Marxist "answer" to the utter collapse of Marxism—and a worrisome indication of how deeply quasi-Marxist themes have sunk into the collective unconscious of the new knowledge class.

Pope John Paul II, for one, is not persuaded.

Centesimus Annus is well worth careful study for its marvelous third chapter alone. For in "The Year 1989," the pope offers a succinct, pointed, and persuasive analysis of the roots of the Revolution of 1989—an analysis whose implications for western societies we ignore at our peril. The fundamental problem with communism or "Real Socialism" was not its economic decrepitude. Rather, communism failed because it denied "the truth about man." Communism's failures were first and foremost moral failures. "The God That Failed" was a false god whose acolytes led societies and economies into terminal crisis.

D. *Yalta Revisited*

Pope John Paul begins his historical analysis of "1989" in 1945, with the Yalta Agreements. "Yalta," in fact, has loomed very large indeed in the vision of the Polish pontiff. World War II, "which should have re-established freedom and restored the right of nations, ended without having attained these goals"—indeed, it ended with "the spread of Communist totalitarianism over more than half of Europe and over other parts of the world." (*CA*, #19.) "Yalta," in other words, was more than a political decision; it was a moral catastrophe and a betrayal of the sacrifices of the war, a betrayal rooted in incomprehension of (or indifference to) the nature of Marxist-Leninist totalitarianism. A failure of moral intuition (or will) led to a failure of politics.

Thus the first truth about Central and Eastern Europe was that the "Yalta arrangement" could not be regarded as merely a historical datum with which one had to deal. Dealing had to be done (not for nothing did Pope John Paul grow up under the tutelage of Cardinal Stefan Wyszyński of Warsaw, a tenacious prelate who gained the Church crucial breathing room in the 1950s). But there should be no illusions. The only "dealing" that would contribute to a genuine peace would be based on the conviction that no peace worthy of the name could be built on the foundations of "Yalta."

As it began, so it would end. The origins of this bizarre and "suffocating" empire found their parallels, forty-four years later, in the ways in which the empire fell.

The moral catastrophe of Yalta was attacked at its roots by "the Church's commitment to defend and promote human rights," by a confrontation with Stalin's empire at the level of ethics, history, and culture. Communism, and particularly communist atheism, the pope said time and time again, was "an act against man." (*CA*, #22.) And the antidote to the false humanism of Marxism-Leninism came from a truly Christian humanism in which men and women once again learned the human dignity that was theirs by birthright.

E. 1979: A Turning Point in Poland

That understanding had never been completely snuffed
out in Central and Eastern Europe. But there was fear—
the glue that held the Yalta imperial system together.
Breaking the fever of fear was thus the crucial first step
in addressing the calamity of "Yalta."

And it seems, in retrospect, that millions of people in
the region—first in Poland, and then elsewhere—began
to face down their fear during John Paul II's first, dramatic return to Poland in June 1979. His message during
that extraordinary pilgrimage was decidedly "prepolit-
ical": It was a message about ethics, culture, and history
devoted to explicating "the truth about man" that Poles
knew in their bones—which was precisely the truth that
their regime had denied for two generations. It was not a
message about "politics" in the narrow sense of the
struggle for power. But it was high-octane "politics" in
the more venerable sense of the term—"politics" as the
ongoing argument about the good person, the good society, and the structure of freedom. And that upper-case
Politics led, over time, to the distinctive lower-case politics of the Revolution of 1989, the revolution that reversed "Yalta."

John Paul II believes that, among the "many factors
involved in the fall of [these] oppressive regimes, some
deserve special mention." The first point at which "the
truth about man" intersected with lower-case politics
was on the question of the rights of workers. The pope
does not hesitate to drive home the full irony of the
situation:

"It cannot be forgotten that the fundamental crisis of systems claiming to express the rule and indeed the dictatorship of the working class began with the great upheavals which took place in Poland in the name of solidarity. It was the throngs of working people which foreswore the ideology which presumed to speak in their name. On the basis of a hard, lived experience of work and of oppression, it was they who recovered and, in a sense, rediscovered the content and principles of the Church's social doctrine." (*CA*, #23.)

That reappropriation of "the truth about man" led to another of the distinctive elements of the Revolution of 1989—its nonviolence. Tactical considerations surely played a role in the choice for nonviolence by what we used to call "dissidents": The bad guys had all the guns, and the good guys knew it. But it is hard to explain why the mass of the people remained nonviolent—particularly given the glorification of armed revolt in Polish history and culture—unless one understands that a moral revolution, a revolution of conscience, preceded the political revolution of '89.

F. *Truth, and a New Form of "Revolution"*

The pope was fully aware that the economic systems of Central and Eastern Europe were in a shambles by the mid-1980s, and that this shambles played its role in the collapse of Stalin's empire. But John Paul also argues that the economic disaster of command economies was not a "technical problem" alone, but rather "a consequence of the violation of the human rights to private initiative, to ownership of property, and to freedom in the economic sector." (*CA*, #24.) Marxist economics, just like Leninist politics, refused to acknowledge "the truth about man."

State atheism in the Eastern bloc also carried the seeds of its own destruction, according to John Paul. The "spiritual void" the state created by building a world without windows "deprived the younger generation of direction and in many cases led them, in the irrepressible search for personal identity and for the meaning of life, to rediscover the religious roots of their national cultures, and to rediscover the person of Christ himself as the existentially adequate response to the desire in every human heart for goodness, truth, and life." (*Ibid.*) The communists, as noted above, had thought that they could "uproot the need for God from the human heart." What they learned was that "it is not possible to succeed in this without throwing the heart into turmoil." (*Ibid.*)

And communism onto the ash heap of history.

John Paul II's discussion of the Revolution of 1989 is carefully crafted, and makes no claims for the Church's role as agent of the Revolution that would strike any fair-minded reader as implausible or excessive. Nor was the Holy See unaware of the many other factors that conspired to produce the peaceful demolition of Stalin's empire: the Helsinki process, which publicly indicted communist regimes for their human-rights violations and created a powerful network of human-rights activists on both sides of the Iron Curtain; the fact of Mikhail Gorbachev; and the Strategic Defense Initiative (SDI), which any number of Vatican officials consider, privately, to have been decisive in forcing a change in Soviet policy.

But in *Centesimus Annus*, John Paul II was determined to teach a more comprehensive truth about the Revolution of 1989—that a revolution of the spirit, built on the sure foundation of "the truth about man," preceded the transfer of power from communist to democratic hands. The Revolution of 1989, viewed through this wide-angle lens, began in 1979. It was a revolution in which people learned first to throw off fear, and only then to throw off their chains—nonviolently. It was a revolution of conservation, in which people reclaimed their moral, cultural, and historical identities. It was a revolution from "the bottom up," the bottom being the historic ethical and cultural self-understandings of individuals and nations.

Which is to say, it was a revolution that reminded the West that a vital civil society was the essential foundation of a democracy.

G. *The Free Economy*

"Not only is it wrong from the ethical point of view to disregard human nature, which is made for freedom, but in practice it is impossible to do so. Where society is so organized as to reduce arbitrarily or even suppress the sphere in which freedom is legitimately exercised, the result is that the life of society becomes progressively disorganized and goes into decline.

"Moreover, man, who was created for freedom, bears within himself the wound of original sin, which constantly draws him toward evil and puts him in need of redemption. Not only is this doctrine an integral part of Christian revelation; it also has great hermeneutical value insofar as it helps one to understand human reality. Man tends towards good, but he is also capable of evil. He can transcend his immediate interest and still remain bound to it.

"The social order will be all the more stable, the more it takes this fact into account and does not place in opposition personal interest and the interests of society as a whole, but rather seeks to bring them into a fruitful harmony. In fact, when self-interest is violently suppressed, it is replaced by a burdensome system of bureaucratic control which dries up the wellsprings of initiative and creativity. When people think they possess the secret of a perfect social organization which makes evil impossible, they also think that they can use any means, including violence and deceit, in order to bring that organization into being. Politics then becomes a 'secular religion' which operates under the illusion of creating paradise in this world. But no political society . . . can ever be confused with the Kingdom of God." (*CA*, #25.)

Pope John Paul II did not hesitate to draw out the implications of his Christian anthropology of human freedom, and his analysis of the dynamics of the Revolution of 1989, in the field of economics. In fact, *Centesimus Annus* contains the most striking papal endorsement of, and challenge to, the "free economy" in a century. The endorsement comes in the form of the answer to a pressing question:

"Can it be said that, after the failure of Communism, capitalism is the victorious social system, and that capitalism should be the goal of the countries now making efforts to rebuild their economy and society? Is this the model which ought to be proposed to the countries of the Third World which are searching for the path to true economic and civil progress?

"The answer is obviously complex. If by 'capitalism' is meant an economic system which recognizes the fundamental and positive role of business, the market, private property, and the resulting responsibility for the means of production, as well as free human creativity in the economic sector, then the answer is certainly in the affirmative, even though it would perhaps be more appropriate to speak of a 'business economy,' 'market economy,' or simply 'free economy.' But if by 'capitalism' is meant a system in which freedom in the economic sector is not circumscribed within a strong juridical framework which places it at the service of human freedom in its totality, and which sees it as a particular aspect of that freedom, the core of which is ethical and religious, then the reply is certainly negative." (*CA*, #42.)

In other words, if by "capitalism" is meant what the West at its best means by capitalism—a tripartite system in which democratic politics and a vibrant moral culture discipline and temper the free market—then that is the system the pope urges the new democracies and the Third World to adopt, because that is the system most likely to sustain a human freedom that is truly liberating.

The defenders of the liberal status quo in the Church

quickly insisted that this endorsement carried a lot of conditions with it. Of course it did—no surprises there. Nor would any thoughtful defender of the market deny the need for its careful regulation by law, culture, and public morality. What is new about *Centesimus Annus* comes in passages like these:

- "The modern business economy has positive aspects. Its basis is human freedom exercised in the economic field, just as it is exercised in many other fields." (*CA* #32.)
- "It is precisely the ability to foresee both the needs of others and the combinations of productive factors most adapted to satisfying those needs that constitutes another important source of wealth in modern society. Besides, many goods cannot be adequately produced through the work of an isolated individual; they require the cooperation of many people in working towards a common goal. Organizing such a productive effort, planning its duration in time, making sure that it corresponds in a positive way to the demands which it must satisfy, and taking the necessary risks—all this too is a source of wealth in today's society. In this way, the role of disciplined and creative human work and, as an essential part of that work, initiative and entrepreneurial ability becomes increasingly evident and decisive." (*Ibid.*)
- "Another task of the State is that of overseeing and directing the exercise of human rights in the economic sector. However, primary responsibility in this area belongs not to the State but to individuals and to the various groups and associations

which make up society. The State could not directly ensure the right to work for all its citizens unless it controlled every aspect of economic life and restricted the free initiative of individuals." (*Ibid.*, #48.)

• "Indeed, besides the earth, man's principal resource is man himself." (*Ibid.*, #32.)

Centesimus Annus thus marks a decisive break with the curious materialism that had characterized aspects of modern Catholic social teaching since Leo XIII. Wealth-creation today, John Paul II readily acknowledges, has more to do with human creativity and imagination, and with political and economic systems capable of unleashing that creativity and imagination, than with "resources" *per se*. And that, John Paul II seems to suggest, is one of the "signs of the times" to which Catholic social thought must be attentive.

H. Rethinking the "Option for the Poor"

In fact, one of the most distinctive characteristics of *Centesimus Annus* is its empirical sensitivity. John Paul II has clearly thought carefully about what does and what does not work in exercising a "preferential option for the poor" in the new democracies, in the Third World, and in impoverished parts of the developed world. The "preferential option," the pope seems to suggest, is a formal principle; its content should be determined, not on the basis of ideological orthodoxy (that is what was rejected in the Revolution of 1989), but by empirical facts. And so far as John Paul was concerned, the evidence is in. What works best for the poor is democratic polities and properly regulated market economies. Why? Because democracy and the market are the systems that best cohere with human nature, with human freedom, with "the truth about man."

It will take some time for this new departure in Catholic social thought to be digested by those committed to what the pope calls the "impossible compromise between Marxism and Christianity" (*CA*, #26), as well as by those who continue to search for a chimerical Catholic "third way" between capitalism and socialism. (At a meeting in Rome, for example, shortly after the encyclical was published, I was informed by the dean of the social science faculty at the Pontifical Gregorian University that "Capitalism A [i.e., the "capitalism" the pope endorses in the paragraph cited above] exists only in textbooks." I privately suggested to the dean, a Latin American Jesuit, that if he really believed that, he had no business running a faculty of social science.) But the text of *Centesimus Annus* itself is plain; the authoritative teaching of the Catholic Church is that a properly regulated market, disciplined by politics, law, and culture, is best for poor people. It works. And it gives the poor an "option" to exercise their freedom as economic actors that is available in no other system.

The implications of this analysis for U.S. social welfare policy are not all that difficult to define. One best exercises responsibility for and to the poor by efforts to include the poor in the free economy and in democratic public life. Empowerment, rather than dependency, is the goal.

I. Culture Wars, Revisited

> "It is not possible to understand man on the basis
> of economics alone, nor to define him simply on
> the basis of class membership. Man is understood
> in a more complete way when he is situated within
> the sphere of culture through his language, his-
> tory, and the position he takes toward the funda-
> mental events of life, such as birth, love, work,
> and death. At the heart of every culture lies the
> attitude man takes to the greatest mystery: the
> mystery of God. Different cultures are basically
> different ways of facing the question of the mean-
> ing of personal existence. When this question is
> eliminated, the cultural and moral life of nations
> are corrupted." (*CA*, #24.)

A good bit of the debate in the immediate aftermath
of *Centesimus Annus* focused, understandably enough,
on the encyclical's careful endorsement of the "free
economy." But the truth of the matter is that John Paul II
is rather more concerned about the "culture" leg of the
politics-economics-culture triad than he is about the
argument between market economists and those still
defending state-centered schemes of development. The
latter debate has been settled. The real issue remains the
ability of a culture to provide the market with the moral
framework it needs to serve the cause of integral human
development.

Once again, the lessons of "1989," for both "East" and
"West," are on the pope's mind. Can the new democracies
develop societies that provide for the free exercise of
human creativity in the workplace, in politics, and in

the many fields of culture without becoming libertine in their public moral life? Will "consumerism"—that is, consumption as an ideology, not as a natural part of what dissidents used to call a "normal society"—replace Marxism-Leninism as the new form of bondage east of the Elbe River? Has it already done so in the West? If not, how can we prevent its triumph? If so, how can we repair the damage and put the free society on a firmer moral foundation?

The pope is not persuaded by libertarian arguments. "Of itself," he writes, "the economic system does not possess criteria for correctly distinguishing new and higher forms of satisfying human needs from artificial new needs which hinder the formation of a mature personality." The market cannot be left on its own, so to speak. "A great deal of educational and cultural work is urgently needed" so that the market's remarkable capacity to generate wealth is bent toward ends that are congruent with "the truth about man"—which is not, John Paul continually urges, an economic truth alone (or even primarily). (*CA* #36.)

In fact, the pope seems convinced that consumerism-as-ideology ought to be blamed, not on the market system, but on the moral-cultural system's failures to discipline the market:

> "These criticisms [of consumerism in its hedonistic form] are directed not so much against an economic system as against an ethical and cultural system. . . . If economic life is absolutized, if the production and consumption of goods become the center of social life and society's only value . . . the reason is to be found not so much in the economic

system itself as in the fact that the entire socio-cultural system, by ignoring the ethical and religious dimension, has been weakened, and ends by limiting itself to the production of goods and services alone." (*CA*, #39.)

But *Centesimus Annus* is by no means a dreary exercise in papal scolding. John Paul II knows that the things of this world are important, and that material goods can enhance man's capacity for living a freedom worthy of a being made in the image and likeness of God. "It is not wrong to want to live better," according to the pope. "What is wrong is a style of life which is presumed to be better when it is directed toward 'having' rather than 'being,' and which wants to have more, not in order to be more but in order to spend life in enjoyment as an end in itself." (*CA*, #36.)

J. Reconstructing Civil Society

So what is to be done? John Paul II is highly critical of the excesses of the welfare state, which, taken *á outrance*, he styles the "social assistance state." Here, the pope argues, is another abuse of human freedom: "By intervening directly and depriving society of its responsibility, the Social Assistance State leads to a loss of human energies and an inordinate increase of public agencies, which are dominated more by bureaucratic ways of thinking than by concern for serving their clients, and which are accompanied by an enormous increase in spending."

John Paul's preference, which is an expression of the the classic Catholic principle of "subsidiarity," is for what, in the American context, would be called "mediating structures": "Needs are best understood and satisfied by people who are closest to [the poor, the weak, the stricken] and who act as neighbors to those in need." (*CA*, #48.) Such mediating structures—religious institutions, voluntary organizations, unions, business associations, neighborhood groups, service organizations, and the like—are the backbone of what Václav Havel and others in Central and Eastern Europe have called "civil society." The reconstruction of this civil society is the first order of business in setting the foundations of democracy—a message that ought to be taken to heart by those in the West, too, especially those who have read their Tocqueville and have pondered the Frenchman's identification of the voluntary association as *the* distinctive and essential institutional foundation of democratic culture in America.

In sum, what is needed is a public moral culture that encourages "life-styles in which the quest for truth, beauty, goodness, and communion with others for the sake of common growth are the factors which determine consumer choices, savings, and investments." (*CA*, #36.) We do not live in hermetically sealed containers labeled "economic life," "politics," and "lifestyle." John Paul insists that it is all of a piece. There is only one human universe, and it is an inescapably moral universe in which questions of "ought" emerge at every juncture; or as the pope puts it, "Even the decision to invest in one place rather than another, in one productive sector rather than another, is always a moral and cultural choice." (*Ibid.*)

As with economics, so with politics. I have stressed here the importance of "1989" in the pope's historical vision. But by "1989," the pope means a set of events fraught with meaning for the West as well as for the East. John Paul II has vigorously positioned the Church on the side of the democratic revolution throughout the world, not because he is a geopolitician, but because he is an evangelist, a moral teacher, and a pastor. The Church, he insists, "has no models to present." But, as an expression of its fundamental concern for "the truth about man," the Church "values the democratic system inasmuch as it ensures the participation of citizens in making political choices, guarantees to the governed the possibility of both electing and holding accountable those who govern them, and of replacing them through peaceful means when appropriate." (*CA*, #46.)

K. Truth and Consequences

John Paul II is almost Lincolnian in wondering whether nations "so conceived and so dedicated can long endure," particularly given the attitude toward the relationship between rights and obligations, between rights and the truth, that one finds in Western cultural elites. It is not as Cassandra but as a friend of democracy that John Paul II lays down this challenge:

> "Nowadays there is a tendency to claim that agnosticism and skeptical relativism are the philosophy and the basic attitude which correspond to democratic forms of political life. Those who are convinced that they know the truth and firmly adhere to it are considered unreliable from a democratic point of view, since they do not accept that

truth is determined by the majority, or that it is
subject to variation according to different political
trends. It must be observed in this regard that if
there is no ultimate truth to guide and direct political activity, then ideas and convictions can
easily be manipulated for reasons of power. As history demonstrates, a democracy without values
easily turns into open or thinly disguised totalitarianism." (*Ibid.*)

Still, the pope continues, "the Church respects the
legitimate autonomy of the democratic order," and the
Church "is not entitled to express preferences for this or
that institutional or constitutional solution." Rather, the
Church is the Church, and thus "her contribution to the
political order is precisely her vision of the dignity of the
person revealed in all its fullness in the mystery of the
Incarnate Word." (*CA*, #47.)

Centesimus Annus is an extraordinary statement of
faith—faith in freedom, faith in man's capacity to order
his public life properly, and above all, faith in God, who
created man with intelligence and free will. It may well
be regarded, in time, as the greatest of the social encyclicals, given the breadth of the issues it addressed, the
depth at which questions were probed, and the empirical
sensitivity John Paul II shows to the "signs of the times"
as they illuminate freedom's cause at the end of the
twentieth century. With *Centesimus Annus*, the "Pope of
Freedom" not only marked the centenary of a great tradition, he brilliantly scouted the terrain for the next
hundred years of humanity's struggle to embody in
public life the truth that makes us free. His is a vision of
the possibilities and the crisis of freedom that Americans,

especially in this season of *Kulturkampf*, most certainly ought not ignore.

Revitalizing the Experiment: Five Truths to Hold

"Translating" the vision of John Paul II into the American context may be difficult politically, but it ought not be difficult intellectually. Indeed, in the work of Father John Courtney Murray, S.J. (1904–67), one of the architects of the Second Vatican Council's Declaration of Religious Freedom, we find an anticipation of John Paul's vision that both coheres with the teaching of *Centesimus Annus* and has much to say to our present circumstances.

Murray believed, with Lincoln (and not unlike John Paul II), that America was a "proposition country"—a political community gathered together by certain ideas and ideals, a political community whose very future rested on the capacity of those ideas and ideals to shape its people's lives. The "American proposition" was composed of truths that the American Founders held in common, truths that were the "inner architecture" of the American experiment in ordered liberty. Moreover, the contemporary vitality of those truths was the key to the successful working-out of our national experiment today. (John Courtney Murray, S.J., *We Hold These Truths: Catholic Reflections on the American Proposition*, New York: Doubleday Image Books, 1964, p. 47; hereinafter *WHTT*.)

Indeed, it is precisely these foundational truths that are being contested in the American culture-war. Murray believed, and I think John Paul II would agree, that the degree to which these truths are "received" in contemporary America and inform the life of the American political community is *the* crucial index of the health of the civil society that sustains our democracy, because unless there is some consensus on the moral architecture of the American experiment, there can be no disciplined public discourse over the ways in which we order our common life. For, as Murray put it, if "barbarism threatens when men cease to live together according to reason. . . . [b]arbarism likewise threatens when men cease to talk together according to reasonable laws." (*WHTT*, p. 25.)

What are these truths? Five of them seem to me most basic, and most urgently in need of reiteration in our present circumstances.

1. The first "truth" on which the American experiment is built—a truth that is first in terms of the ontology of the experiment as well as in terms of its functional aspects—is the truth that God is sovereign over nations as well as over individuals.

This truth distinguishes the American tradition (a conservative tradition, in the sense of maintaining continuity with the central political tradition of Christian Europe) from the Jacobin/laicist tradition of late-eighteenth century continental Europe and its nineteenth and twentieth-century epigones. In the latter tradition (which gave rise, *inter alia*, to the Reign of Terror as practiced by both Robespierre and Lenin), the "autonomous reason of man" was "the first and the sole principle of political organization." (*WHTT*, p. 40.) In the American revolutionary tradition, conversely, the sovereignty of God, which necessarily stands in judgment on all our works, is the first principle of political organization.

This theological affirmation has critical public consequences. Because God is God, Caesar is not God. Because Caesar is not God, politics is not ultimate but, at most, penultimate. The affirmation of God's sovereignty over the nation as well as over the individuals who compose it is thus a crucial barrier against succumbing to the totalitarian temptation. The affirmation of God's sovereignty over the nation also sets limits on the boundaries of the political, even as it invests politics with its own proper dignity.

Moreover, because God is sovereign, all the works of our hands—and especially those works of our hands that have to do with the exercise of power—are under judgment. When we pledge allegiance to the flag today and affirm "one nation, under God," we reaffirm the Founders' notion that the nation—the American experiment in ordered liberty—is "under judgment." The organization of the experiment, and the laws by which the experiment is conducted, are to be judged against a larger moral horizon than that of immediate political expediency or interest.

This is not a truth that is well understood in, say, the Supreme Court today. But the recovery of this foundational understanding is perhaps the key to a revitalization of the American experiment that is in moral continuity with the Founding.

2. The second truth on which the American experiment rests is the truth that man has the God-given capacity to be self-governing.

In other words, the God who gave us life and liberty also gave us the capacity to reflect on our circumstances and to discern from that reflection our moral obligations. The social embodiment of this truth about the human person is, Murray argued, the notion of a "free people under a limited government"—the best shorthand formula, he believed, for the essence of the American experiment.

According to that familiar formula, government is not simply coercion. Government is "the right to command"; government is authority, and its authority is both derived from law and limited by law. (*WHTT*, p. 43.) Thus the notion of the "rule of law" ought not be understood, Murray wrote, in the positivist sense that the law is simply what the law says it is. No, the law, too, is "under judgment." The law is to be judged by moral criteria that transcend it.

Here, too, is an issue on which a renewed conversation is imperative in contemporary America, most especially in terms of the controversies over abortion and euthanasia. The fact that a right-to-life movement is thriving in the United States, twenty years after the principal culture-forming institutions of our society pronounced the issue settled on behalf of a radical abortion license, is powerful testimony to the "reception" of Murray's second truth by millions of Americans—even as the resistance to that movement in the academy, the media, many churches, and much of the permanent political class (a resistance increasingly mounted on the basis of "autonomy" claims) illustrates the depth and gravity of the culture-war.

3. The third truth on which the American experiment rested, in Murray's analysis, was the truth that just governance—governance that is congruent with the dignity of human beings as persons, as moral agents—is by, through, and with the *consent* of the governed.

This was, Murray argued, an ancient principle, with deep roots in the political thought of Christian medieval Europe (which, of course, was shaped by Roman law and Greek political philosophy). But in the American experiment, the ancient principle of consent was married to another principle—the principle of popular participation in governance. (See *WHTT*, p. 45.)

Thus Lincoln's phrase at Gettysburg, "government *by* the people," was no mere rhetorical flourish. The people adopted their basic law, the Constitution, through elected representatives. The people made the laws of the land through other elected representatives and rotated the executive power such that the Constitution came "alive" in the rhythms of our national life. In short, as Murray put it, "the people are governed because they consent to be governed; and they consent to be governed because in a true [but not mechanical] sense, they govern themselves." (*Ibid.*)

All of which raises serious questions today, of course, about the rise of a permanent political class, the role(s) of the media in public life, and the conditions of civic education—questions which bear heavily on the conduct of the American *Kulturkampf*.

4. It hardly needs saying that Murray's third truth involves a real act of faith in the capacity of the people, not to settle technical minutiae, but to wrestle seriously with great issues. That faith was, in turn, built on Murray's fourth truth, the fourth building block in the intellectual/moral foundations of the American experiment—the truth, again medieval in root, that "there is a sense of justice inherent in the people" by which they are "empowered to judge, direct, and correct the processes of government." (*Ibid.*)

This truth took concrete political form in the First Amendment's guarantees of free speech and a free press. In Murray's view, these freedoms were not rooted in the thin individualistic claim that someone has a right to say what he thinks just because he or she happens to think it.

Rather, these freedoms had a thicker reality; they were social, *public* necessities. For, as Murray argued, people who are required to obey first have the "right to be heard" about the matters on which their obedience is to be required; and people who bear burdens and make sacrifices have the right to debate and pass judgment on whether the policy requiring those sacrifices in fact serves the common good. (*WHTT*, p. 46.)

These rights, and the fourth truth that they express, give concrete reality to the fundamental distinction between *society* and the *state*, and embody the traditional Western Christian understanding that "society" is morally and, one might say, ontologically *prior* to the state. This means, in practical, daily terms, that the state exists to serve society, not the other way around. That understanding, revived in Central and Eastern Europe during the 1970s and 1980s under the rubric of "civil society," played a crucial role in the collapse of communism, as we have seen. But it is also the foundation, in our American context, of the freedom from governmental control enjoyed by the academy, the means of communication, and, most urgently, by the family and by religious institutions. Nor is it an accident that legal encroachments on the independence of those "prior" institutions (especially church/synagogue and family) are among the most fevered issued in the American *Kulturkampf*—which, yet again, shows itself to be an argument down to first principles.

5. The fifth truth on which, Murray believed, the American experiment rested was the classic claim that "only a virtuous people can be free." (*WHTT*, p. 47.)

Like the Founders, and like Pope John Paul II, Father Murray understood that free government in a free society is not inevitable, only possible, and that its possibility can only be realized *publicly* when the people are governed *inwardly* by the "universal moral law." Or, as Lord Acton put it, freedom is "not the power of doing what we like, but rather the right of being able to do what we ought." (*Ibid.*)

On this understanding, of course, and to come straight back to the beginning, democracy is more than a political experiment, more than the "Rules of the Game." No, democracy is a spiritual and moral enterprise, and its success (or failure) depends upon the virtues (or lack thereof) of the people of the enterprise. As Murray argued, men and women who would be free must learn to discipline themselves, and the governing institutions of a free society must be self-governing "from within" if they are to serve the ends of virtue—and of freedom. (*WHTT*, p. 48.)

Thus the American ideal, on Murray's understanding of the Founders' intention—an intention congenial to classic Catholic understandings of man, society, and history—was not simply freedom, but ordered freedom: freedom ordered from within by the virtues of the people, and ordered from without by constitutional and positive law that holds itself accountable to the same transcendent moral law that is the ethical compass of each individual citizen.

It would be foolish optimism, bordering on culpable naiveté, to suggest that these five truths are "held" in American society today, such that our public discourse and our public life are consistently disciplined by reference to them. But the very fact of the American *Kulturkampf* is itself an interesting witness to the continuing vitality of this ensemble of fundamental affirmations.

For the denial of these truths by those intellectual, political, and legal forces that would reduce (and traduce) American democracy to a framework for the pursuit of the gratification of the Imperial Self has led to their rediscovery in some quarters (primarily Roman Catholic), and their discovery in others (primarily evangelical Protestant).

We cannot know the result of the American *Kulturkampf* with any certainty. But the experience of Weimar Germany stands before us as a grim warning: The most elegantly constructed democratic institutions will crumble and fall when the moral tissues of civil society decay. We may not hold "these truths" as firmly today as they have been held in the past. But we fail to grasp them at our peril, and at the peril of the American experiment itself.

CORPPORATE SOCIAL RESPONSIBILITIES IN THE NINETIES

by

Richard S. Lombard

Richard S. Lombard

Richard S. Lombard is Of Counsel to the law firm of Baker & Botts in the firm's Dallas, Texas, office. He recently retired as a Vice-President and as General Counsel of Exxon Corporation, a position he held for nearly 20 years.

Born in Panama, in the former Canal Zone, he graduated from Harvard College in 1949 and from Harvard Law School in 1952. After receiving his law degree, he was associated with the firm of Haight Gardner Poor and Havens in New York City. He joined the law department of an Exxon Corporation affiliate in 1955 and served in a number of positions in Caracas, New York, Houston, and Dallas.

Mr. Lombard is a Director of the American Arbitration Association and formerly Chairman of the Association's Board of Directors and Chairman of the Board of Supervisory Trustees under the will of Edwin B. Parker, which has fiscal and oversight responsibilities for the Parker School of Foreign and Comparative Law at Columbia University. He is past Chairman of the Advisory Board of the International and Comparative Law Center of The Southwestern Legal Foundation in Dallas and is a Trustee of the Foundation. He is also a member of the American Law Institute, the American Bar Association, and other professional organizations and is the author of American–Venezuelan Private International Law, a Bilateral Study, *published by the Parker School of Foreign and Comparative Law in 1965.*

CORPORATE SOCIAL RESPONSIBILITIES IN THE NINETIES

by

Richard S. Lombard

Over the course of the twentieth century, business corporations have become the dominant institutions of our economic structure. Most Americans view corporations with respect, and nearly all of us accept them as necessary for the maintenance and continued growth of our standard of living. Some of us are suspicious of these large and seemingly impersonal organizations of great economic power. But as the century nears its end, most of us have concluded, perhaps reluctantly in some cases, that the unmatched ability of large corporations to raise investment capital and their productive efficiency bring benefits we cannot do without today.

The American public and business corporations have come to terms. Big business may have its lobbyists and its layoffs, its plant closings and mergers and high executive salaries, provided it does its work in ways that satisfy the public's expectations. It is clearly understood that the public's expectations will change from time to time, and it is up to business corporations to conform. Those that do not will suffer community disapproval, and may ultimately go out of business.

The public's expectations as to conduct define the social responsibilities of corporations. Many of these expectations are set forth in law, which in a democracy reflects some of the public's standards. Other expectations, equally and sometimes more exacting, are unwritten, and enforced by economic and political sanctions more powerful than law.

What does the American public expect of corporations today, in the last decade of the century? How have these obligations changed in past decades, and how might they change again? How have corporations adapted to past changes, and how should they adapt to new ones?

In our country today, the chief social obligations of a business corporation are three: first, to provide goods or services that people want to buy at prices they are willing to pay; second, to reinvest in the business for the future; and third, to do all of this at a profit sufficient to give those who have financed the corporation an acceptable return on their investment.

These are not all; there are additional major obligations to obey the laws, to deal fairly with employees, and to carry on business in ways that protect the integrity of the environment and the safety of the public. In wartime, at least during popular wars, there is an obligation to cooperate with government policy in support of the war effort. And of course there is the important obligation to contribute to educational, cultural and charitable causes in the community.

These obligations, in my opinion, reflect most of today's widely-held public expectations in the United States as to corporate conduct. Some argue for additional social responsibilities not yet part of the consensus. One might say that a socially responsible corporation should not manufacture certain products, such as cigarettes, liquor, or firearms. Another might argue that it should eschew certain businesses, such as nuclear energy. There is a variety of such views, some contradictory, all based on the moral standards and expectations of their advocates, and some with the potential for earning wide public acceptance and thus someday becoming obligations enforceable by law or public opinion.

The three principal obligations—to provide people with goods or services at prices they are willing to pay, to reinvest for the future, and to operate at a profit acceptable to investors—are so fundamental that a business cannot long survive if it fails to meet them.

The intensity of the public's expectation that corporations supply desired goods or services at acceptable prices is not always evident. Usually, if a single company fails to provide acceptable goods, or prices them too high, customers buy from a competitor. But if alternative supplies are not available, the customers take offense.

The oil industry knows this better than most. In the very early 1970s, minor and temporary shortages of motor gasoline supplies led to expressions of public dissatisfaction with the oil industry's ability to meet the needs of its customers. There was reciprocal resentment among some elements in the industry. I remember seeing bumper stickers in Texas that said "Let the Yankees Freeze in the Dark." This was the modern equivalent of Commodore Vanderbilt's famous saying: "The public be damned." It did not reflect the attitude of responsible managers of oil companies, who knew better than to provoke the wrath of the public, but it did reflect a woeful misunderstanding on the part of a few people of the power of public opinion.

Within a very short time, the situation got much worse. In the winter of 1973–1974, most of the Arab oil exporting countries, including Saudi Arabia, imposed an embargo on crude oil exports to the United States and the Netherlands, and subsequently reduced production volumes, for reasons having to do with the Arab conflict with Israel. There was a sharp drop in crude oil supplies in the United States, and in some parts of the country there were serious shortages of motor gasoline. People waited in line for hours to buy fuel. The moral indignation of the public, the press, and the politicians was ferocious. Oil executives were publicly insulted and harangued by senators and congressmen, and newspaper and television criticism of the industry was vitriolic. It was wrongly asserted that the oil companies had conspired with the Arabs to create shortages to justify increases in prices. The reaction of Congress was to impose punitive taxes and additional price controls on the industry, and the industry's reputation in the public eye was permanently damaged.

Other industries have had similar experiences. The lesson is very clear: business corporations must do all in their power to supply the goods and services people want, and to keep prices within an acceptable range. If they fail, for whatever reason, whether culpable or not, the public will take its revenge.

Another major responsibility of business corporations is reinvestment: building new and replacement plants and wells and mines and machine tools, as well as supporting research, invention and development of new technology, improved products, and new and better ways of delivering services. A business that does not reinvest and renew itself will gradually, or sometimes suddenly, disappear. Even the neighborhood grocery store must replenish its wares every day, and maintain and replace and upgrade its cold storage compartments, its air conditioning, its parking lots and grocery carts and cash registers. (It is hard to find a large supermarket today that does not use bar code readers at check-out counters, with enormous savings in labor costs and reduction in waiting-in-line time for customers.) A large oil company must do the same on a colossal scale, as producing wells run dry and refinery vessels corrode with time and use. And constant effort and ingenuity and resources must be used to maintain the quality of products and the efficiency of production and delivery at least at the level of competition. As the population grows, business corporations must grow too, to provide the additional goods and services for more people. Customers, shareholders, lenders, suppliers, employees, annuitants, and future generations all rely upon the business corporation to stay in business by reinvestment.

The idea that business corporations have an obligation to society to operate at profit levels satisfactory to their investors is not self-evident, and some do not accept it. Some say that there is a tension between business morality and ethics, on the one hand, and business necessity on the other. In that view, the board of directors and officers of a corporation are thought to be constrained in their moral choices and ethical decision-making by a sordid desire to make profits. That is the view of those who criticize business for, as the critics put it, "valuing profits above principles." It assumes that the pursuit of profits is at best morally neutral. Other critics of business go further, and assert that the pursuit of profits not only lacks moral justification but is actively immoral in itself, and that those who engage in it are reprehensible.

Another perspective on that view is held by some businessmen and women themselves, who feel guilty about what they perceive as a subordination of their better moral natures to the imperatives of commerce, and are somewhat ashamed of their occupations.

There is a refreshing wind of understanding today of the social necessity of the pursuit of profit by corporate management. The sudden and dramatic collapse of communism in Europe and the former Soviet Union, and the brave efforts of the new leaders of former communist states to implement market economies in place of state socialism, have shown the world the social value of the profit motive. Even in some of the remaining communist countries, including China, the social utility of the profit motive has belatedly been recognized. A considerable amount of free enterprise is being permitted Chinese citizens and foreign investors, and its beneficial effects on the economy are already being appreciated.

Here in the United States, there is a new interest on the part of pension funds and other large and powerful institutional shareholders in the profitable conduct of business by the corporations in which they own shares. In times past, a shareholder disappointed in the profits and dividends of a company would follow the famous Wall Street rule: If dissatisfied with the way a company is managed, sell your shares. A number of circumstances have been changing. Institutional shareholding has grown enormously, so that today some half or more of the stock of some of the largest corporations is owned by a relative handful of major owners, principally private and public employee pension fund trustees. At the same time, faith in index investing has become widespread. Index investing is the system by which very large investors spread their investments across all of a large group of stocks, such as the Standard & Poor's Composite Stock Price Index, in proportion to their market valuations, so that the market value of their total portfolio fluctuates up or down precisely as does the S&P 500 or other index average. The philosophy of index investing is inconsistent with the Wall Street rule: One cannot own stock in all of the S&P 500 if one sells the stock of those companies with whose management one is dissatisfied. Today, instead of selling underperforming stocks, these major investors often seek to influence, or if need be to replace, underperforming managers. The trustees of pension funds, themselves fiduciaries for the retirees and their families who depend upon their pensions for survival, expect the same standard of fiduciary conduct by the directors and officers of the companies in which they invest. If it is not met, they may insist upon dismissals and new appointments.

The moral basis of the obligation of directors and officers to operate the business profitably, and the concomitant obligations to reinvest for the future and to provide goods or services at prices people will pay, is similar to the obligation of a trustee. The trustee is obligated, morally and legally, to invest and manage the trust's assets in the best long term interests of the widow and of the children who are the beneficiaries of the trust. The obligation of the corporation's directors and officers is to manage the business in the best long-term interests of all those who depend upon it: the owners, the lenders, the employees, the annuitants, their families, the suppliers, the customers, and the people in the communities where the corporation carries on its business. This is not a principle of economics devoid of moral underpinning: It is a moral obligation itself. To fail to meet it can bring heartbreak and misery to real people.

To illustrate, consider a hypothetical large corporation in the computer business. (Let me interject that I am

not describing I.B.M. While there may be elements similar to I.B.M.'s situation, I.B.M.'s problems are much
more complex than the simple situation we will hypothe-
size.) This hypothetical corporation was widely regarded
as having an exemplary record of ethical and responsible
corporate citizenship. It was among the first American
corporations to withdraw from business in South Africa,
and it had an exceptional record of hiring, training, and
promoting women and minority employees. It had
several women and blacks on its board. It was among the
first companies to provide on-premises child care for
employees, and voluntarily gave parental leaves. It was
well known for its generous support of the arts and education and science. Its employee relations policies were
extraordinary. Although the corporation employed hun-
dreds of thousands for many decades, no employee had
been involuntarily laid off. If a plant or division had to be
closed, the employees were offered generous severance
allowances and enhanced pension benefits if they chose
to leave, but if they preferred to stay, they were given
other assignments, with relocation and retraining at
company expense if necessary. In short, the corporation
was, or appeared to be, a splendid example of a business
being conducted in accordance with the highest community standards.

Now this hypothetical corporation had pioneered the
development of computers and had built its enormous
business primarily upon large mainframe computers.
Let us suppose, however, that its management had failed
to anticipate the rapid development and popularity of
personal computers and the speed and extent to which
they would supplement mainframes in many applica-
tions. Let us suppose that even as unprecedentedly large

numbers of employees became surplus to the company's needs due to these changes in the marketplace for computer services, the company held to its long-standing no-layoff policy, at heavy cost.

The predictable consequences came rapidly. As demand for the company's products fell, revenues declined, but without a proportional decrease in labor expense. The company suffered losses, the stock price declined, and the board was forced to reduce the dividend. The company's bonds were down-rated, resulting in drastic declines in their market value and greatly increased interest costs to the company for future borrowing.

The company had long encouraged employee stock ownership. A hundred thousand or more retired employees, who relied upon their company stock value and their dividends, saw their incomes greatly reduced and their security imperilled. Current employees with long years of dedicated service saw their future prospects of promotion and even of continued employment dimming. Since it was too late to start new careers elsewhere, many had no choice but to stay with the company even as it became a less and less desirable place to work. Many sought other employment, but a worldwide recession made other jobs difficult to find. College plans for many employees' children were deferred indefinitely. Many suppliers of components and services to the corporation were necessarily cut off as the corporation's business grew smaller, and their owners and employees faced similar problems. Some went into bankruptcy.

These calamities were in large part attributable to grievous errors of the hypothetical company's management. They failed in their primary obligations to manufacture a product that people would buy at a price they were willing to pay, to renew the company's product line in anticipation of future demand, and to generate profits that would give investors an acceptable return on their investments. All of the grants to museums and public television that had burnished the company's once shining reputation for good corporate citizenship were of no consolation to the employees, annuitants, suppliers, and others who were suffering.

Each of us can think of real-life stories that are similar to this hypothetical case. Consider the American automobile manufacturing companies that gave their employees and annuitants enormously expensive comprehensive medical coverage, fully paid for by the companies. Once they were applauded for their generosity and social conscience; now some face shocking losses, and survival is not assured. While there are many causes for their financial problems, one of the most important is the high cost of medical benefits. General Motors' medical benefits cost the company an average of $1,500 a vehicle.

And this leads to consideration of the moral and ethical responsibilities of the automobile workers' unions that extracted those medical benefits from the manufacturers by threat of strikes. The manufacturers chose to agree to the medical benefits rather than accept the consequences of strikes. It is fair to attribute a share of the moral responsibility for the present state of the American automobile industry to the automobile unions. The unions saw their responsibility only to their current members, and failed to see that future generations of automobile workers might be laid off, or never be employed at all, if the auto companies' costs became a crushing burden which could not be sustained. Similar examples of errors by both management and labor can be found in the steel industry and elsewhere.

A series of recent business losses, and subsequent management changes brought about by independent directors with the support of pension funds and other major shareholders, have refocused attention on the obligation of management to operate the business at a profit. The moral climate is changing. More and more now realize that there is a social obligation to say no on occasion, that there is a social obligation to be sure that the costs of doing business are not out of line with those of present and potential competitors, both at home and abroad, and that there is a social obligation to operate a business at a decent profit for the benefit of those who will otherwise suffer.

Another major social obligation of corporations is to obey the law. The relationship between law and moral values has engaged the thoughts of scholars, theologians, judges, and philosophers for generations. There have been times in the history of this country when some laws were widely regarded as so immoral that they should be disobeyed. Even today, the laws of some foreign countries are viewed as immoral by American standards, and American businesses are castigated for compliance with those foreign laws by their foreign subsidiaries, as we will discuss in a moment. Today, federal and state laws of our country affecting business are generally respected, and probably reflect the moral standards of most of the people. Society demands compliance.

The obligation to obey the law is very broad. It includes the important obligations imposed by private civil law, such as living up to contractual commitments and avoiding wrongful acts that cause injury, death, or property damage. It also includes compliance with public law, such as antitrust laws, income tax laws, food and drug labelling and testing laws, and laws relating to issuance and trading in stocks and bonds.

It is occasionally said that the obligation to obey the law includes compliance not only with the letter but also with the spirit of the law. This is sometimes true, but not always. Few expect a taxpayer to pay more tax than the letter of the law requires, even though the "spirit" of the tax law can be said to be to raise revenue for the government. The Internal Revenue Service sometimes criticizes what it calls "abuse," which often means nothing more than a taxpayer's taking lawful advantage of the technical provisions of our very complex tax code and regulations. And the "tax loopholes" decried by partisans are nearly always provisions of the law intentionally enacted by Congress to favor some kinds of activities over others in terms of their tax consequences. Society's remedy for loss of government revenue due to such causes is to amend the law prospectively.

In other important areas, though, corporations that observe only the letter of the law risk more serious adverse consequences. An excessively narrow and technical view of the law's requirements, or an assertion of right under a too-literal reading of a contract, can invite retribution by judges, juries, or legislatures or severe consumer reaction. The possibility of such sanctions in effect broadens the law's requirements and increases the penalties for noncompliance. There are many examples; one is the frequent imposition of liability upon banks for damages suffered by borrowers when the banks call demand notes or terminate lines of credit where clearly permitted under the strict language of their contracts but held to be in "bad faith." Managers of business corporations must decide which laws need be complied with only to the letter and which must be construed more broadly to avoid society's disapproval.

How does a corporation obey the law? Corporations are not animate. They do not act, they do not reflect, they do not think, and they do not choose. Their directors, officers, employees, and agents, all human beings, make choices and decisions and take actions which the law attributes to the corporations. An unlawful act by one single employee out of a hundred thousand total employees, no matter how low his level, if done in the course of employment, can make the corporation responsible for huge criminal fines or civil penalties and damages. Of course the employee may also be liable, but it is the corporation which has the resources to pay the damages or the fines. This vicarious liability, penalizing the shareholders of the corporation for acts for which they have no personal responsibility at all, is presumably imposed by society in order to force corporations to do everything in their power to see that their employees obey the law.

Every major corporation should have, and most do have, a written policy of compliance with law and a program of education and enforcement of that policy within its organization. Such a policy statement, issued by the board of directors, is an essential beginning. Then it must be made known to every employee in the organization, and made known through management channels, so that the employee in the small sales office in a city distant from headquarters knows that his local supervisor is personally committed to the policy just as much as the president and the directors of the corporation. The widespread publicity given to the Ten Commandments

is not enough to ensure that thousands or tens of thousands
of employees will understand that the corporation wants
them to comply with the law and that they will be fired if
they do not. The directors and officers should set an
example of strict compliance with law and high standards of ethics in their own conduct, both on the job and
in their personal affairs. There must also be a system for
monitoring compliance, for detecting violations, and for
discipline of violators, and there must be constant education and re-education of employees as to the provisions
of law most likely to be applicable in their respective
parts of the organization. Sales managers need instruction in the antitrust laws against price fixing. Plant
managers need to know the law as to employee safety and
disposal of toxic substances. Directors need to know the
law as to permissible and impermissible mergers and
acquisitions. Shop foremen need to know the law prohibiting sexual harassment. These educational efforts,
usually carried on by lawyers in the corporation's law
department, are rightly called preventive law. Preventive law is a continuous challenge because new employees
arrive every day and because laws change often. And in a
multinational corporation, the laws to be observed are
not only those of the United States, but also of the European Community and the various countries where the
corporation does business.

Compliance with the law by American-owned subsidiaries operating in foreign countries is not simple. While
there are usually more similarities than differences in
the laws of the United States and of the host country, the
differences can be major. For example, U.S. law prohibits employment discrimination on the basis of race,
religion, and sex. The laws of some foreign countries

require employment discrimination on such grounds. For the most part, U.S. law and public opinion stop at the water's edge and do not put American-owned foreign subsidiaries in the impossible position of having to comply with inconsistent social expectations and laws. But at the end of the day, an American-owned corporation must always comply with its obligations at home, even if this means it must sell or close down a foreign subsidiary. This is what happened to American businesses in South Africa, most of which were unable to continue operating there in compliance with South African laws on apartheid when their parent companies at home were subjected to ever-increasing social, financial, and legal pressure from the American public. Most American-owned South African subsidiaries were sold.

Another obligation of the modern American business corporation is to treat employees fairly. Fairness takes on different meanings when public opinion and law change, as they do often and rapidly in this important field. As this talk was being written, Congress was considering a law to prohibit the employment of permanent replacements for striking workers, and there was a public debate on that issue. The Americans with Disabilities Act has only recently become effective; it is likely to result in many more employment opportunities for the disabled. There is a trend toward the adoption by industry of compulsory arbitration, instead of litigation in court, of employer-employee disputes of all kinds, not limited to employees represented by unions.

Consider the changes in the moral climate in the United States with respect to sex discrimination against women in employment matters. In 1963, only thirty years ago, employment discrimination against women in hiring was not prohibited by federal law. Although some state laws prohibited it, such discrimination was widespread. Newspaper classified ad columns showed jobs available for men and jobs available for women. Many employers limited employment in certain occupations by sex, and many labor unions limited membership in the same way.

This form of discrimination was not generally regarded as immoral. On the contrary, it was often seen as positively moral, on the grounds that giving a job or a place in the union to a woman took away a job from a man who had a wife and children to support. Also, the view was commonly accepted that children were best off being raised by a mother at home, where she could not be if she had a job.

Those arguments for discrimination against women have not wholly lost their force today, but they are no longer preeminent on the battleground of ideas. Today, the leading idea is that women, like men, have a right to pursue occupations and professions if they wish to do so, without regard to the interests of their own spouses or of their own children, much less the interests of other families. The stark clarity of that view is illustrated by a recent Supreme Court decision holding that a corporation could not prohibit pregnant women and women of childbearing age from working in an area of the plant where exposure to lead might endanger unborn children.

Whether or not this idea of equality of opportunity for women is ever universally accepted, even in the United States, it has been enacted into federal law since the Civil Rights Act of 1964, which applies to both employers and labor unions. This law is enforced, with considerable vigor at times, and has been effective in opening many new jobs and careers to women.

Large business corporations and labor unions today have no real choice but to comply with the Civil Rights Act as to the initial employment and admission to membership of women who meet employment or membership standards. Once a woman is employed, however, her progress within a business organization is determined less by the dictates of the law than by the way she is perceived by her supervisors and other managers within the company. The perception of qualifications for promotions and transfers is necessarily more and more subjective as an employee rises in the ranks, and more and more difficult for judges, juries, and government officials to second guess. It is in these more complex choices that the moral factor becomes as important or more important than the law in influencing decisions.

One large group of employers, U.S. government contractors, are subject to additional legal pressure through the so-called affirmative action obligations imposed upon them by the government. They are required to establish goals and timetables for the promotion as well as for initial employment of women and members of racial minorities and are at least in theory subject to suspension or debarment from government business if they do not.

The law and these regulations stop short of requiring fixed quotas for women and members of minority groups at particular job levels, and so it is difficult to measure compliance. A manager who is unsympathetic with the objective can find ways to delay and deflect the implementation of goals and timetables. But if the board of directors and principal officers of the corporation are truly determined to see women rise to occupy higher and higher positions in the business, they can make it happen.

How they can make it happen is worth examination. It is much more difficult to effect major personnel policy changes within a business corporation than it might seem from outside.

One way to achieve the objective of, say, having women as one quarter of the corporation's vice presidents is to discharge the necessary number of men and appoint women in their places. This is more or less the way the present administration in Washington is increasing greatly the number of women and minority group members in high level federal positions. Of course it is relatively easy for them to do this, since all of the Republican incumbents of those positions resigned after the presidential election.

It is not likely that any corporation's board of directors believes that its business could withstand the shock of such a draconian step. But what about the alternative of filling top level positions with women as they are vacated by attrition, as male incumbents resign or retire or die?

Here the board has a more difficult decision. When the vice president in charge of engineering retires, will there be a woman engineer with sufficient professional and supervisory skill and experience to fill the job? Will she be as well qualified in these respects as the three or four men who have been working up through various levels of responsibility in manufacturing, sales, and engineering for twenty years and who all have outstanding performance ratings? If she is not perceived by others in the organization as the professional equal of the other candidates, will her promotion result in a wave of resignations, a decline in morale, and subtle resistance to her as a supervisor, which will make her ineffective?

It will be seen that the process of preparing women to make them eligible for high level jobs must begin at the first level of promotion, and must be carefully planned and implemented over a long time. Patience is required. It usually takes twenty or more years of appropriate experience to be ready for promotion to vice president in a major company. Not many women entered the pipeline twenty or twenty-five years ago. As a single example, take Kay Bailey Hutchison, the newly elected Senator from Texas. She graduated from the University of Texas law school in 1967, one of only seven women in her graduating class. Today, one-third or more of the law school graduating classes each year are women, and twenty-five years from now the much bigger pool of women candidates will make it much easier to find one qualified for promotion to vice president and general counsel of a big company than it is to find a qualified woman today who graduated twenty-five years ago.

The process of development of women candidates for future high positions must be accompanied by educational measures to be sure that their peers and others in the organization, both men and women, understand that the board of directors is determined that promotions will be made on the basis of merit, without regard to sex. This can be done in a number of ways. Factors for consideration in evaluation of job performance can specifically include sensitivity to equal opportunity in employment. A vigorous and well-publicized program to prevent sexual harassment can be instituted, and offenders discharged to show the seriousness of the offense. And at every opportunity, well-qualified women must be promoted to intermediate steps along the ladder to give evidence that the corporation means what it says.

The corporation's social obligations as to safety and environmental responsibility include as a minimum compliance with applicable laws, but the scope of the obligations is much broader than the laws' requirements. Compliance with law is not enough. Under the federal Superfund law, for example, corporations and others who in the past lawfully turned over wastes to licensed haulers for disposal are now retroactively labelled as "polluters" and may be required to pay part or all of the cost of remediation of old waste disposal sites where the materials were deposited. They were in full compliance with the law when they in good faith handed over the waste materials, which often at that time were not generally regarded as hazardous at all, but standards have changed, and now they must pay.

Another indication of the extraordinary degree of public concern for the environment is the enactment by Congress of criminal laws and the increasing prevalence of criminal prosecution for environmental offenses. Corporations can be heavily fined and branded as criminals for simple negligence of low level employees causing environmental damage. In some cases, there have been criminal convictions based on strict liability laws, where there is not even evidence of negligence. If an airline pilot is careless and causes a crash that kills a hundred passengers, there is no basis for a criminal prosecution, but if an oil tanker captain is careless and grounds the tanker, spilling oil that injures no one but kills sea birds, both the shipowner that employed the captain and even the cargo owner are subject to criminal prosecution and enormous fines. These are facts of life today, and corporations are spending a great deal of effort and money in environmental and accident protection measures.

There are limits, however, to what a corporation can do to meet increasing expectations of environmental protection and to withstand the costly delays in securing all of the many environmental permits that are now required before a new mine or plant can be built. One way corporations can adapt to impossible barriers and licensing delays in this country is to close or phase out their operations here and open new ones in countries where standards are different from ours and jobs and the prospect of earning foreign exchange from export sales are valued more highly than environmental protection. This is happening in the mining industry. In the last two years, mineral exploration in the United States declined 13 percent. It doubled in Latin America. The president of a well-known American mining company was quoted recently in the *Wall Street Journal*. He said, "A U.S. mining company has to go international or it runs a very high risk of going out of business."

Let me add that I am neither deploring nor endorsing the high value placed upon environmental protection today by the American public, nor the high value placed on jobs and exports in some other countries. I am only observing that public expectations are not the same in every society, and that a corporation can sometimes respond to changing public standards in one country by moving its operations to another.

Some would question the morality of such a decision and suggest that an American corporation has an obligation to maintain its operations in the United States regardless of regulatory difficulties, low profits, or even losses here. This is a position often asserted by or on behalf of American labor unions, in an effort to retain jobs in this country. There is force to this view, and it should not be lightly ignored by corporation management. But it is not, or at least not yet, a generally accepted position. Most people would agree that an American corporation is free to invest abroad if opportunities there look better than those at home, although some would agree reluctantly.

During the Second World War, American business corporations were expected to do all they could to cooperate with the nation's war effort. Nearly all did so with a will, and their managements and employees could be justly proud of their contributions to victory. Building ships, bombers and tanks was the right thing to do, and the public approved.

It is instructive to contrast this public approval with the opprobrium heaped upon Dow Chemical Company during the Vietnam War because it manufactured and supplied our army with napalm, a deadly and effective weapon of fire, which had been developed during World War II and used against Japanese fortified islands during the Pacific campaigns. The Vietnam War's opponents in this country singled out Dow as a target for sit-ins and sabotage because of its napalm manufacture. Nothing had changed except public opinion.

There is not yet a consensus in our country that business in peacetime should always follow the policy laid down by the administration in office. In general, corporations listen carefully to what the President and his cabinet officers say but do not always comply with their wishes, unless of course those wishes are expressed in mandatory regulations or taken to Congress and made law. This can give rise to tension. Corporations whose businesses affect a great many consumers must be very sensitive to the risk of Presidential approval, as must corporations whose businesses are unusually dependent upon government favor or tolerance. A large airline company would fit both of these categories. It is no small thing for any company to ignore a White House or cabinet request, but in our country, unlike some foreign nations, business corporations are not generally expected to act as instruments of state policy.

Contributions to educational, cultural, and charitable organizations are also widely regarded today as a social obligation of business corporations. This was not always so. It was only forty years ago that the Supreme Court of New Jersey, in a landmark decision, held that it was appropriate for a business corporation to give away a small part of its funds to Princeton University on the grounds that educational and charitable gifts indirectly benefitted the corporation's shareholders. Today, every large corporation has a planned program of gifts and grants for such purposes, particularly focused on the communities where it has plants, offices, and employees. Few today challenge the propriety of such corporate generosity.

These philanthropic programs cost relatively little, but they are extremely important to a corporation's reputation for good citizenship in the United States. Charitable and educational gifts are favored by the federal income tax law and are fully deductible by corporations. By contrast, European business corporations make relatively few charitable and educational gifts in their own countries although their subsidiaries in the United States follow the same policy as American corporations. European subsidiaries of American corporations also give away relatively little. Such contributions are not usually tax deductible in Europe, reflecting a different public view of the desirability of corporate philanthropy. The general European view appears to be that education and charity are the responsibility of the state, not of business. In this respect as in others, it is public expectations that determine the obligations that corporations have to society.

What changes in public expectations are likely to affect business corporations in the next decade?

The three fundamental obligations—to provide goods or services the public wants at prices the public will pay, to reinvest for the future, and to operate at a profit—will not change as long as we have a capitalist economy. There will no doubt be more demonstrations of the public's moral disapproval at unexpected scarcity of an essential product or service, as happened during the Arab oil embargo. There is little that business corporations can do to anticipate such problems, except to be sure they do not cause them themselves. The insurance industry, for example, can be vulnerable to public retribution if too many insurance companies stop insuring the same risk in the same state at the same time.

It is possible, but fortunately not certain, that we will all learn an expensive lesson in the need for business to operate at a good profit if the federal government imposes price controls on an important industry, such as pharmaceuticals. There is a real possibility that the dramatic research achievements of the pharmaceutical industry in recent times will be slowed or stopped by public policy measures intended to control health costs.

As to the obligation to obey the law, business corporations must redouble their compliance program efforts in the light of the new federal sentencing guidelines, which will result in even greater criminal fines, but which also provide for a partial reduction in fines if the corporation has in place a well-designed compliance program.

In the area of employment fairness, it is possible, but not likely, that the idea of comparable worth will gain public acceptance and be forced upon corporations. Comparable worth is an idea whose time has not yet come, in our country, in terms of public and legislative acceptance. The idea behind it, to oversimplify, is that the wages of a worker should be determined by social scientists rather than by the marketplace. Social scientists, employed by the state, would determine the "worth" of, say, a nurses aide's job in relation to the "worth" of an ambulance driver's job, taking into account such factors as necessary educational background, required skills, and working environment. If they conclude that the jobs are of equal worth, the hospital would be required to pay the same wages to both groups, even though the prevailing wage rates for the two groups in the relevant community might be different. The public at large in the United States is not yet persuaded that comparable worth studies should determine wage levels, instead of the market. Comparable worth policies have been adopted for public employees in a few places, but not yet for employees of business corporations. However, the province of Ontario has enacted comparable worth legislation for private employees, and the idea may someday move to this country.

A more likely development in the general view of fairness to employees will be the continuing trend of state laws and court decisions that are gradually moving most states away from the notion of employment at will and toward broad legal protection of the employee's job. "Employment at will" means that an employee can be fired at any time for any reason, or indeed for no reason.

This was at one time the law in many states, but it is less and less so every year. Very recently, for example, New York, which was long a strong employment-at-will state, enacted a law that prohibits firing an employee for any lawful conduct outside the work place. In time, the risks of damages for wrongful discharge of employees, including punitive damage awards, will become so great that business may consider seeking legislation like that in many foreign countries, where a discharged worker is entitled to a fixed payment, based on a years-of-service formula, when discharged for almost any reason. This may prove less expensive in the long run than jury verdicts.

There is no doubt that we will see more and more laws, and more and more heavy fines and penalties, in the environmental area. It is possible that there will be new laws and increased use of criminal sanctions for other accidents as well, especially if there is a well-publicized disaster that calls the public's attention to the safety risks presented by some industries. One area of great vulnerability for business corporations is the risk of accidents caused by employees under the influence of drugs or alcohol, and particularly as to employees who are thought to be recovering alcoholics or drug abusers. Under one view of present law in this country, at least as interpreted by the Federal Equal Employment Opportunity Commission, a pilot cannot be refused a place in the cockpit of an airliner because he was once an alcoholic, and most airlines comply with this law. Exxon Shipping Company restored the captain of the Exxon Valdez to his position after he had been through a program of rehabilitation for alcoholics. But when his subsequent relapse and drinking allegedly contributed to the Prince William Sound disaster, Exxon was vilified, sued, and prosecuted criminally. Exxon has since adopted a new policy that bars former alcoholics and drug abusers from safety sensitive positions. Predictably, Exxon is now being sued by the Equal Employment Opportunity Commission, which asserts that the new policy unlawfully discriminates against the handicapped. I don't know which side will win the suit, but I think it is only a question of time until there is another serious accident, this time costing human lives, which may bring about a change in the public's view of the proper balance between compassion for unfortunate former alcoholics and addicts and the safety of the public.

Corporate philanthropy seems likely to be a social obligation of business for a long time to come. If the proportion of the student population enrolled in public universities continues to increase, it is possible that this trend will in time reduce the need for corporate gifts to independent universities. The great English universities were for centuries supported by religious and private donations, but today receive most of their support from the government. On the other hand, many public universities in the United States, including the University of Texas at Dallas, receive a large proportion of their total support from corporate contributions, and recent changes in the federal income tax law have reduced tax deductions for charitable and educational gifts made by some high-income individuals, but not for those made by corporations. There is also a growing need for supplemental financial support for primary and secondary schools, which now receive little assistance from corporations.

We cannot be sure what changes there will be in public expectations when we enter the next century, but we can be certain of change. Wise business managers will look ahead and plan for change. They must listen to the young people who will soon speak with authority. They must pay attention to critics as well as to friends of business. They must seek every opportunity to tell the public what their corporations are doing already to meet the public's demands and expectations. They must do what they can to help see that the public is informed as to scientific, technical, and economic imperatives and choices that should be taken into account in establishing public standards. And above all they must be flexible, for when change comes it can come quickly, and corporations must move quickly to adapt to it.

PLURALISM AND CIVIL SOCIETY: THE CHANGING CIVIC CULTURE

by

James A. Joseph

James A. Joseph

James A. Joseph is President and Chief Executive Officer of the Council on Foundations. The Council is a national organization of more than thirteen hundred foundations and other grantmakers whose assets total more than ninety billion dollars.

President Clinton nominated him to be the Chairman of the Board of Directors of the Corporation for National and Community Service, and the U.S. Senate has confirmed the nomination.

Mr. Joseph came to the Council on Foundations in 1982 after a distinguished career in government, business, and education. He was the Under Secretary of the Interior from 1977 to 1981, and a Vice President of Cummins Engine Company and President of the Cummins Engine Foundation from 1972 to 1977. His degrees are from Southern University and Yale. He has taught at Yale and Claremont and served as a Visiting Fellow at Nuffield College at Oxford University.

Mr. Joseph also taught at Stillman College in Tuscaloosa, Alabama, where he was a leader in the local civil rights movement. An ordained minister, he was also Chaplain of The Claremont Colleges in Claremont, California, and a member of the faculty of the School of Theology.

In 1977, Mr. Joseph was appointed Under Secretary of the Interior by President Jimmy Carter. Mr. Joseph was a member of the Advisory Committee to the Agency for International Development under President Reagan and was appointed an incorporating director of the Points of Light Foundation and a member of the Presidential Commission on Historically Black Colleges by President Bush. He often represents the United States abroad.

Mr. Joseph is a member of the Council on Foreign Relations and the Overseas Development Council. He serves on the Board of Directors of The Brookings Institution, Colonial Williamsburg Foundation, the National Endowment for Democracy, Africare, and the Children's Defense Fund.

Mr. Joseph is the author of The Charitable Impulse, *a study of wealth and social conscience in communities and cultures outside the United States. He has contributed to a number of other important books and published a wide variety of articles. He is also the recipient of numerous honorary degrees.*

PLURALISM AND CIVIL SOCIETY:
THE CHANGING CIVIC CULTURE

by

James A. Joseph

The historical concept of the American society is that of a people forming a more perfect union, a society that is neither fixed nor final, a nation that is always in the making. It is still true, as Thomas Paine wrote in *Common Sense*, that "we have it within our power to begin the world all over again."

Yet, many of our citizens seem to fear the present remaking of America. The argument over what constitutes a national identity has led to a breakdown of civility, with zealots of all sorts clinging tenaciously to old myths out of fear that some of their most cherished fictions might be discarded or discredited.

I want, thus, to argue that diversity need not divide, that the fear of difference is a fear of the future, that pluralism rightly understood and rightly practiced can be a benefit rather than a burden. I want to suggest that despite the polarization of our society, indeed, the balkanization of our world, there are reasons to be optimistic about the potential for coherence and community. For years, we thought we could find common ground in a shared political culture. More recently, we turned to the economic culture. But I am persuaded that it is in the civic culture that we find the shared values that can provide healing and wholeness in a badly fractured world.

Three ideas are converging to create a new civic culture that is at one and the same time both local and uni-

173

versal. The first is the idea of a civil society, that cluster of ideas, ideals and social arrangements through which a people find their voice and mobilize themselves for a common good. Around the world people are using very similar language to describe very different expressions of their yearning for opportunity and advancement. But whether they appeal to the civic idealism of Locke, Rousseau, Hegel, or de Tocqueville or the moral values of Jesus, Buddha, Mohammed, or Moses, there is increasing belief in the importance of maintaining an intermediate space between the individual and government where private energy can be spontaneously developed and deployed for a common good. **It is for many people in many parts of the world a new way of thinking.**

The second is the idea of a good society, the notion that a good society depends as much on the goodness of individuals as it does on the soundness of government and the fairness of laws. In the last few years, I have been to Eastern Europe, Central America, and Southern Africa, and everywhere I have gone, I have found people taking matters into their own hands because they have come to believe that while some governments in some parts of the world are working well for some of their people, few governments anywhere in the world are working well for all of their people—especially those on the margins. They are seeking to transform the laissez-faire notion of live and let live into the moral imperative of live and help live. **It is for many people a new way of acting.**

The third is the idea of a transforming society, the notion that when neighbors help neighbors and strangers help strangers, both those who help and those who are helped are transformed. Civic engagement provides a new perspective, a new way of seeing ourselves, a new understanding of the purpose of the human journey. People around the world are finding out that when that which was "their" problem becomes "our" problem, the transaction transforms a mere association into relationships with the potential for new communities of meaning and belonging. **It is for many people a new way of being.**

Let us examine each of these ideas in more detail, beginning with the notion of civil society.

Civil Society

While its precise meaning is still evolving, the principles and practices in which the concept is anchored now seem to enjoy almost universal acceptance. One can trace the roots of civil society in Western thought back to Aristotle and Cicero, but it is most prominently associated with more recent political philosophers.

John Locke emphasized the rights and duties of citizens. Thomas Jefferson and others borrowed from him the idea that these rights included life, liberty, and the pursuit of happiness. But Locke's notion of civil society was in many ways restrictive and exclusionary. John Stuart Mill, on the other hand, was interested in a more inclusive society. He extended the idea of rights to include women and working people who did not own property. He was interested not only in maintaining the privileges of freedom, but in expanding the benefits as well. Georg Wilhelm Hegel, who may have been the most prominent in developing the concept of civil society, saw its main feature in the existence of intermediate or mediating institutions between an individual and the state. Alexis de Tocqueville did not define the term in his famous study of *Democracy in America,* but he described a system of voluntary organizations that we now associate with the notion of a civil society.

What strikes me in reviewing Western political thought is that the meaning of civil society is still evolving not only abroad, but here in the United States as well. But despite the many cultural roots that have given life to the concept, what the devotees of civil society seem to share in common is a set of values that is grounded in at least four principles: (1) the idea that citizens have rights and responsibilities that precede the state, and the true patriot is the one who is willing to protect his country from even his own government; (2) the idea that society is distinct from government and that government is but one of several sectors that can, and should, promote the common good; (3) the idea that a healthy society is one that protects the freedoms of speech, of the press, of assembly, and of worship; and (4) the idea that the rights of the minority are to be protected by the majority.

This is the environment in which our efforts to build and sustain community will take place in the final years of our transition to a new century. It will be, in many ways, the age of ethics, as our society moves away from the notion of ethical relativism, where ethics was a person's own business, to the notion of a global culture where ethics is everybody's business. The common ground is the primacy of individual freedoms, the protection of human rights, the centrality of intermediate or mediating institutions, and the commitment to an open, plural, and equitable society.

It would be a mistake to assume, however, that our society or our tradition has an exclusive claim to these values. If we are to find coherence in the new civic culture, we must acknowledge and celebrate the myriad traditions that honor liberty and hail freedom. As a United States Senator told a journalist several years ago, the people who are forming new societies in Eastern Europe and elsewhere do not sit around reading the *Federalist* papers or have a conversion experience on the road to Damascus. Everywhere I go, I find people asking not which political philosophy is the purest, but what practices are likely to be the most humane, what procedures are likely to be the most just, what systems are likely to be the most effective.

A Good Society

All of which brings us to the idea of a good society, the notion that there is in each of us the urge to connect with another person and to provide solace, comfort, and aid. We have seen in recent years a resurgence of the Hobbesian idea that human beings are moved chiefly by the desire for power and other selfish considerations. The view of the English philosopher Thomas Hobbes that human beings are by nature self-centered and uncaring overlooks the many people in unlikely places who choose every day to go beyond normally expected standards of civic duty and public obligation.

But the problem of building and sustaining community in our time goes much deeper than even Hobbes supposed. It is one of the ironies of our age that as communities around the world are becoming more alike—with our economies more interdependent and our lifestyles, values and aspirations more similar—people are more and more turning inward, seeking to return to smaller, more intimate forms of community.

This may appear at first glance to be a contradiction, but I am convinced that it is a natural part of the search for common ground, a search which involves, first and foremost, a search for beginnings. The more humanity sees itself as inhabiting a single planet, the greater the need for each culture on the globe to assert a unique heritage.

Despite our emphasis on the melting-pot version of national identity, there has never been a time when Americans looked exactly alike, spoke the same language, or believed the same thing. This has never been a totally homogeneous community; whatever cohesion early Americans enjoyed, much of it was based on mutual respect, and that, not surprisingly, is today's missing element. Unless mutual respect is restored, our cities will continue to unravel. Real communication will be impossible and real community unlikely.

I would be remiss if I did not point out that this need for respect begins with our different histories. Those who decry the affirmation of ethnic identity and the use of history as a therapeutic tool overlook the fact that history has always been therapeutic. It provides the resource for dignity and the capacity for self-assertion. While we must insist that it be accurate and inclusive, it is in the nature of the craft that those who write history will be influenced by their own story.

There is an old African proverb that says, "If lions had historians, tales of hunting would no longer glorify the hunter."

While I don't want this lecture to sound like a sermon, I cannot help but recall the remarkable observation of Dietrich Bonhoeffer, the German Protestant theologian executed by the Nazis. He wrote from prison in 1942 that he had learned to see the great events of world history from below, from the perspective of those who are excluded, under suspicion, ill-treated, powerless, oppressed, and scorned—in short, those who suffer. The controversy last year surrounding the historic voyage of Columbus reminded us that American history would be different if it were written from the perspective of those who were ill-treated, oppressed, and scorned—in short, those who were the victims: the Native Americans who saw 90 percent of their population destroyed, the Japanese Americans who were systematically gathered up and relocated to prison-like enclaves, and the African Americans and Latinos whose difference in status has been treated as a difference in kind.

It is right and good that winners tell their story, but like Dietrich Bonhoeffer, we need to learn to see the great events of world history from below as well. And this is why racial minorities are now claiming as Fortinbras did to Horatio in *Hamlet*, "I have some rights of memory in this kingdom." While there are shrill voices making inaccurate and unrealistic claims in every community, it would be a mistake to permit them to drown out the many authentic voices whose only bias is toward accuracy rather than advocacy. Despite the disclaimers of those who have used history to serve parochial purposes, it is still possible to honor one's history without dishonoring the history of others.

Howard Thurman, the African American theologian, was fond of saying "I want to be me without making it difficult for you to be you."

So if my first point is that there will be no social cohesion, no authentic community, until there is respect for our difference, my second point is that the new pluralism makes demands that the old pluralism never anticipated.

But what does it mean to speak of a new pluralism? Most of us have seen, at one time or another, statistics on the changing social, economic, and ethnic profile of the American communities, but I wonder how many of us have considered the demographic implications of life in an increasingly interdependent world. According to the World Development Forum, if you lived in a representative global village of 1,000, there would be

- 564 Asians
- 210 Europeans
- 86 Africans
- 80 South Americans
- 60 North Americans

There would be

- 300 Christians (183 Catholics, 84 Protestants and 33 Orthodox)
- 175 Moslems
- 128 Hindus
- 55 Buddhists
- 47 Animists
- 210 without any religion or confessed atheists
- 85 from other smaller religious groups

Of this group

- 60 would control half the total income
- 500 would be hungry
- 600 would live in shantytowns
- 700 would be illiterate

It is thus no surprise to find many people, in many parts of the world, asking what is the genesis of community. Is there a common ground, a social glue, a civic ethic that transcends countries and cultures, religion and race?

When Alexis de Tocqueville wrote about the uniqueness of the American society, half a century after the
founders had pledged to form a more perfect union, he
thought he had stumbled on to the unifying element—
civic participation. He mused about everyone's "taking
an active part in the government of society." But a
century and a half later Robert Bellah, lamenting the
decline of civic participation, warned of the threat of a
democracy without citizens. His concern was not so
much with a threat to democracy as it was with the potential decline in the civic infrastructure that makes
democracy viable.

Another foreigner and keen observer of American life
was Gunnar Myrdal, the Swedish economist and sociologist, who wrote *The American Dilemma*. He saw the
unifying element as "the American creed," that cluster
of ideas, institutions, and habits that affirm the ideals of
the essential dignity and equality of all human beings, of
inalienable rights to freedom, justice, and opportunity.
Others have found the potential for common ground in
America's civil religion, but the Protestant ethic that
once undergirded it is waning. James D. Hunter, who
teaches the sociology of religion at the University of
Virginia, is but one of many voices who argue persua-
sively that the civil religion that once united America is
dead. He sees, instead, an increasing conflict over fundamental conceptions of moral authority; conflicts over
different ideas and beliefs about truths, the good, obligations to one another, the nature of community, and so
on. Dr. Hunter describes these conflicts as "culture
wars" further polarizing an already polarized society.

The idea of a unifying American creed is obviously in
trouble. The bonds of social cohesion and community are

increasingly fragile. Moral theologians, political philosophers, and opinion leaders of all sorts are once again in search of common ground. Yet, it may be that they have been simply looking in the wrong place, assuming that the American creed was a fixed and final orthodoxy.

I have been examining the benevolent traditions of America's minorities as part of my research for a book on Visions of Community, and I have found many common elements that can be used to affirm and advance the connectedness of humanity. Not only do they provide the basis for a new American creed, but they point to civic values and civic habits shared in common with America's majority.

We are still romanticizing the good days when social cohesion and civic solidarity came from a common race, a common religion, or a common culture, when neighbors came together to build each other's barns. But those who analyze demographic and social trends are telling us that the community of the future is likely to be a dynamic process in which strangers meet, discover their commonality, deal with conflicts, and celebrate their unity while still remaining strangers. What this suggests, then, is that our notion of community must change conceptually, from the paradigm of a network of neighbors to the metaphor of a company of strangers.

Our notion of community is also changing functionally. In the past, we have spoken of our communities as divided among three sectors: a public sector driven by the ballot, a private sector driven by profit, and a voluntary sector driven by compassion. But the functional boundaries of community are increasingly ambiguous with the most productive sector for solving social problems being what Peter Drucker has called the fourth sector of private/public partnerships.

Solving the problems of our time will require the efforts of all of us, working through private as well as public institutions and profit as well as nonprofit organizations. Our response to the tinderbox atmosphere in our cities has been too long like a cartoon I recall from the *Los Angeles Times* in the 1960s. It was a picture of a boat with a hole in the middle with two groups huddled on each side and someone saying, "Gee, what a nasty leak; thank God it's on the other side of the boat." It is time for policy makers and opinion leaders to remind us that we are all in the same boat and any leak anywhere is likely to sink us all together.

A Transforming Society

So we come to the third and final idea which could significantly change the way in which we meet social needs and solve social problems. If the focus on civil society has to do with civic vitality—widening the circle of community—and the focus on a good society has to do with civic values—stretching the horizons of the heart, the idea of a transforming society has to do with civic vision, the capacity to see connections, to focus on the future, understand it, interpret it, and lead others to help create it.

The most compelling vision of community still comes from John Winthrop's notion of a city on a hill in which we delight in each other, seek to make the condition of others our own, rejoice together, labor and suffer together, always having before our eyes the individuals in our community as members of the same body.

When you experience the problems of the really poor or troubled, when you help to develop or maintain excellence in theatre or dance, when you help someone to find cultural meaning in a museum or creative expression in a painting, when you help someone to find housing or regain his health, you are far more likely to find common ground. And you are likely to gain a sense of personal satisfaction and meaning in the process.

So each of us needs to make some form of involvement in behalf of the neighbor a part of the human journey. Robert Kennedy was fond of saying that few of us have the greatness to bend history, but each of us can change a small portion of events. I believe that many of you in this audience have the power to bend history itself.

Let me, thus, conclude with several observations coming from my own experience in business, education, and government that has enabled me to cope successfully with a changing world while retaining my basic values.

(1) If you seek power, seek it to disperse it rather than simply to concentrate it. Use your power to activate power in others.

(2) If you choose to challenge the establishment, challenge it from within as well as from without. Remember that the engines of fundamental change often are to be found in the old and the orthodox as well as the new and the unorthodox.

(3) Know your history and take pride in your heritage, but use it to liberate the soul, not to enslave the mind. Remember Camus' definition of a true rebel as one who knows what he is for altogether as much as what he is against.

(4) Use your values not so much to proclaim absolutes as to help cope with the ambiguities. In times of rapid change, zealots emerge claiming one truth and one theology, but it is still true that we see through a glass darkly.

(5) Develop the capacity for humility. Remain open to the possibility of human error on your part and human wisdom in unexpected places. Be humble without being docile, aggressive without being an aggressor.

I am thus reminded, as I conclude, of the Greek mathematician, Archimedes, who is reported to have said, "Give me a lever long enough and I can move the world." I would argue that those of you who are assembled for this lecture are part of the fortunate ones who have been given the lever. I hope you will go out and move the world.

MULTICULTURALISM AND POLITICAL RESPONSIBILITY

by

Jean Bethke Elshtain

Jean Bethke Elshtain

Jean Bethke Elshtain, Centennial Professor of Political Science and Professor of Philosophy at Vanderbilt University, is a political philosopher whose task has been to show the connections between our political and our ethical convictions.

A graduate of Colorado State University (A.B., 1963), Professor Elshtain went on to earn a Master's degree in history as a Woodrow Wilson Fellow before turning to the study of politics. She received her Ph.D. from Brandeis University in politics in 1973 and immediately joined the faculty of the University of Massachusetts/Amherst. She became a full professor in 1981. She joined the faculty of Vanderbilt University in 1988. She has also been a visiting professor at Oberlin College and Yale University.

Professor Elshtain has been a National Endowment for the Humanities Fellow at the Institute for Advanced Study, Princeton University. She currently serves as a member of the Board of Trustees of Members of the Institute for Advanced Study. She has been a Scholar in Residence, Rockefeller Foundation Bellagio Conference and Study Center, Como, Italy; a Guggenheim Fellow (1991–92) working on an intellectual biography of Jane Addams; and a Writer in Residence, MacDowell Colony, Petersborough, New Hampshire.

Her books include Public Man, Private Woman: Women in Social and Political Thought *(1981),* The Family in Political Thought *(editor, 1982),* Meditations on Modern Political Thought *(1986),* Women and War *(1987),* Women, Militarism, and the Arms Race *(co-editor, 1990),* Rebuilding the Nest: A New Commitment to the American Family *(co-editor, 1990),* Power Trips and Other Journeys *(1990),* Just War Theory *(1990),* But Was It Just: Reflections on the Morality of the Persian Gulf War *(co-author, 1992).*

She is the author of seventy essays in scholarly journals, eighty or more essays in journals of civic opinion, and some one hundred book reviews and has delivered many guest lectureships.

MULTICULTURALISM AND POLITICAL RESPONSIBILITY

by

Jean Bethke Elshtain

We've all seen them—the World War II films in which the airplane crew or the platoon has a group of guys, all GIs and all proud of it, with names like LaRosa, O'Brien, Goldberg, Chavez, Olafsen, Mickwiecz. They're Americans to the man, and they are making a point—we're different from the people we are fighting. America is a universal identity in the sense that it is open to all comers. You don't have to be of a particular race, or adhere to a given religion, or bear an identifiable ethnic name from one of a small handful of accepted groups to be one of us. The picture isn't perfect—by no means. You don't see an African American or a Japanese American in the group. The Armed Forces were segregated until after the second World War, and Japanese Americans fought in a separate Nisei regiment. But the point could be taken nonetheless: America was different because we provided for the different to hold something in common—their identity as citizens, their aspirations as free men and women, their determination to make life better for their children. That seems a rather long time ago, doesn't it? A frozen tableau from another time and place. A time when we were innocent, perhaps, or naive, or just "didn't get it" in today's harsh jargon.

Maybe. But I don't much like the way we have "wised up," for it seems that rather than growing wise we have, in fact, grown cynical. And that isn't so smart. A free society cannot long survive widespread cynicism among its citizens. Cynicism breeds a politics of resentment. A politics of resentment drains our normative institutions, including education and politics and even the family, of their overriding ethical legitimacy and deters them from doing the tasks they are there to do. The reading of the text of a World War II war film, in today's current jargon, would probably go something like this: Men from various ethnic groups were violently forced to conform to the model of the hegemonic, phallogocentric, dominant Anglo-Saxon Protestant male, save for those the society even more violently refused to normalize, namely, blacks and, in this era, Japanese Americans. Having encoded this dominance more generally, such men, already oppressors in their own households by virtue of their superior standing in a patriarchal society, became ever more eager embodiments of the normative standards of a racist, sexist, imperialist society. End of story.

I exaggerate a bit—for comedic effect or shock value, depending upon how familiar the reader is with the current coinage of the academic marketplace—but not by much. For we are now enjoined to see the past in harsh and dismissive terms: Christianity is nothing but the violent reincoding in new guise of the violent Jewish God; the American Constitution is nothing but the writing into law of the privileges of a dominant, male class; Abraham Lincoln, as one mightily exercised soul shouted at me after a lecture I had delivered, should never be quoted because he was nothing but a racist. The relentless drumbeat goes on. We more and more find criticism—trashing, as it is called—as an end in itself. But I worry about this willful contempt for the past. Such contempt stokes arrogance, fuels the flames of historicist prejudice. The sad thing, of course, is that much of what I here decry is undertaken in the name of putting things right, of correcting some wrongs, of celebrating what is called "multiculturalism," defending it against all hegemonic normalizers everywhere.

But in this matter as in so many others, things are not necessarily what they claim to be. I propose that we take a closer look at this new multiculturalism. What do its proponents assume? What do they claim? What do they aim for? What are the effects of these aims and claims on citizenship and responsibility in a free society? Let me begin to answer these and other questions by reminding us, once again, of what is at stake. There are, it seems to me, two false and dangerous stories about multiculturalism and American identity. The first is drawn from a historical era, now past; the second from the present moment. I will rehearse these two tales that pose or posed particular threats to the generous dream of democracy as the way free citizens come to know a good in common they cannot know alone.

My first cautionary tale is the story of a quest for unity and homogeneity that assaulted diversity in the process: A too strong and overreaching homogeneous identity was deemed necessary as a prerequisite for citizenship and responsibility. Let me take the reader back, for a few brief moments, to the World War I era when the allure of an overarching, collective civic purpose took a statist turn that seemed a cure for what ailed the republic, at least in the view of those who lamented our excessive diversity. Nationalizing progressives, disheartened at the messy sprawl that was American life and desirous of finding some way to forge a unified national will and civic philosophy, saw the coming of World War I as a way to attain at long last a homogeneous, ordered, and rational society.

"To be great," wrote John R. Commons, a progressive labor economist, "a nation . . . must be of one mind." (Cited, as are subsequent quotes on this era, except where noted, from David M. Kennedy, *Over Here: The First World War and American Society,* [Oxford University Press, 1980.]) Walter Lippmann assaulted the "evils of localism" and fretted that American diversity was too great and had become a block in the way of order, purpose, and discipline. World War I was to be the great engine of social progress with conscription, in historian David Kennedy's words, an "effective homogenizing agent in what many regarded as a dangerously diverse society. Shared military service, one advocate colorfully argued, was the only way to 'yank the hyphen' out of Italian-Americans or Polish-Americans or other such imperfectly assimilated immigrants." President Wilson, who had already proclaimed that any "man who carries a hyphen about him carries a dagger that he is ready to plunge into the vitals of the Republic," thundered, in words of unifying excess:

> "There are citizens of the United States, I blush to admit, born under other flags, but welcomed under our generous naturalization laws to the full freedom and opportunity of America, who have poured the poison of disloyalty into the very arteries of our national life. . . . Such creatures of passion, disloyalty, and anarchy must be crushed out. . . . The hand of our power should close over them at once."

"Americanization" became the goal, the watchword; for some, the threat—one nation indivisible. To be sure, genuine regard for the welfare of immigrant groups lay at the base of much progressive sentiment, the fear that separatism and heterogeneity were synonymous with inequality and marginality. But progressive and liberal opinion proved particularly susceptible to the cry for unity because of its stress on the notion that the voice of the nation must speak as one. The temptation to forge a unity that is nigh indistinguishable from stifling conformity is great; it invited figures from Woodrow Wilson down to trim the sails of free speech on the grounds that the war against dissent was a war against civic dismemberment, a war for great national aspirations, and an opportunity to forge a community that might encompass the entire continent. The coming of the first World War offered to this particular progressive mindset an optimistic set of "social possibilities." (For the full story of this move to what I tag "armed civic virtue," see my *Women and War*, Basic Books, 1987.)

It should be noted that American education, from the elementary through the college level, was enlisted in this effort. For the first time, a national curriculum was endorsed, an approved course of study that allowed for little ambiguity. For example, something called the National Board for Historical Service set itself up to reject or accept commissioned syllabi for history courses, often rejecting those that raised doubts about the "positive values of nationalism." America's institutions of higher learning went for the war with relish. The dream of unity—not, I submit, a democratic dream—had become national.

Perhaps, then, current practitioners of the "hermeneutics of suspicion" are right. Perhaps the entire thrust of American history has been to destroy our particular identities, even our dignity, in order to create some common identity, some homogenized product. There is, of course, as in all distortions, a kernel of truth to such claims. But it not the truth of the matter unadorned. For even in the midst of the rush to yank the hyphens out, there were dissenting voices. One was that of Randolph Bourne, himself a member of the progressive crowd and a regular correspondent for *The New Republic* until he fell out with the publishers over their newfound war fervor. Bourne wrote a wonderful piece at the height of war suspicion and fanaticism and attacks on aliens and immigrants. Bourne championed a "trans-national" society. He yearned for a politics of commonalities that cherished and celebrated the bracing tonic that perspicuous contrasts offer us to the forging of individuals and communities. He called for an experimental ideal in which each of us is free to explore in a world in which we are also responsible for others, where we can act in common together and act singly.

This Bournian ideal, if I may call it such, is necessarily hostile to any overly robust proclamation of American identity that demands a single, overarching collective unity, under the aegis of the state, to attain or to sustain its purposes. But his ideal also alerts us to a second false and dangerous story. For the vision Bourne lifts up for our consideration also stands in opposition to proclamations in the name of diversity and multiculturalism that codify and rigidify difference, that reduce us to ethnic, racial, or gender categories, that celebrate a harsh particularism cynically dismissive of the possibility for reaching outside one's own group. This second false story is a perversion of the dream of democracy and the education and civic life constitutive of it.

Bourne celebrated a cosmopolitan enterprise, a world within which many voices were heard. "America," he wrote, "is coming to be, not a nationality but a transnationality, a weaving back and forth, with other lands, of many threads of all sizes and colors. Any movement which attempts to thwart this weaving or to dye the fabric any one color, or disentangle the threads of the strands, is false to this comopolitan vision." (Randolph Bourne, "Trans-national America," in *The Radical Will: Randolph Bourne. Selected Writings 1911-1918*, Urizen Books, 1977, p. 262.) No "tight and jealous" nationalism for Bourne, rather the vision of many threads woven to form unexpected patterns—not of a quilt with solid patches representing this color, this gender, and this or that identity, all kept separate and threatening at any moment to detach itself from the quilt. Thus his vision also serves as an alternative to the rigidifying of difference now underway in many places in American civic life and education.

A problem is this: Once a victimization ideology takes hold, an ideology that exculpates the victim from responsibility for his or her actions, and this ideology is tied to a militant vision of multicultural identity, democracy is in deep peril, a peril greater, perhaps, than that presented in the World War I era. For in that epoch, dissent from the polemics of the overzealous nationalizers came from many quarters, including within the ranks of the Progressives themselves, those who were most enthusiastic about the war's centralizing potential. I've mentioned Randolph Bourne. The great Jane Addams was another, breaking ranks with her colleagues, including one of her heroes, John Dewey, over the war and the overheated, intolerant rhetoric that mowed down whatever stood in its pathway. By contrast, criticism now tends to be severed along lines of sharp ideological cleavage; indeed, criticism of multiculturalism is itself sufficient to throw one into the ranks of reactionaries, according to defenders of multiculturalism. Thus the debate within liberal ranks is far more anemic than it ought to be. This dereliction of critical duty is a worry, but it is not my worry for the purpose of essay. Rather, I will now turn to a more specific case against a politics of difference that undermines democratic possibilities.

What is happening more and more is this: Rather than negotiating the complexity of public and private identities and embracing the notion of "the citizen" as the way we have to sustain a public identity not reducible to the terms of our private selves, we are told that we must gain recognition along race, gender, and sexual preference lines. The public world is a world of many "I's" who form a "we" only with others exactly like themselves. Democrats historically would have found this peculiar at best; anathema at worst. We recognize in the rush for recognition a powerful, and legitimate, modern concern. Some forms of equal recognition are surely not only possible in a democracy but form its very life blood. The question is—what sort of recognition? Recognition of what? For what? To claim, "I am different, you must recognize me and honor my difference," tells me nothing, nothing at all. Should I honor someone, recognize her, simply because she is female or proclaims a particular version of her sexual identity? This makes little sense. I may disagree profoundly with her about everything I find important—from what American policy ought to be in the war in the Balkans, to what needs to be done to stem the tide of deterioration and despair in

America's inner cities, to whether violence on television is a serious concern or just an easy target for riled and worried parents and educators.

My recognition of her difference—by which I mean by preparedness to engage her as an interlocutor, given our difference on the things that count politically, namely, equality, justice, freedom, fairness, authority, power, and so on—turns on the fact that I share something with her: She is in the world with me; she, too, is a citizen. We both bear responsibilities to, and for, our society. We both, I hope, operate from a stance of good will and an acceptance of the backdrop of democratic constitutional guarantees and democratic habits and dispositions, including a commitment to rough and ready parity and an energetic desire to forge at least provisional agreements on highly controversial issues and, if we cannot, to remain committed nonetheless to the centrality of dialogue and debate to our shared way of life. If I am her enemy—because I am white or a heterosexual or a mother or an academic—her only desire can be to silence me, to reproach me, or to wipe me out. One makes war with enemies; one does politics—democratic politics— with opponents. (This paragraph and several others are drawn from my Massey Lectures for the Canadian Broadcasting Corporation, delivered in November 1993.)

The question of the one and the many, of commonality and diversity, has long vexed political thinkers in the West. The American Founders were well aware of these vexations. They worked with, and against, a stock of metaphors that had previously served as the symbolic vehicles of political incorporation. As men of the Enlightenment, they rejected images of the body politic that had dominated medieval and early modern political thinking. For a Jefferson or a Madison, such metaphors as "the King's two bodies" or John of Salisbury's twelfth-century rendering, in his *Policraticus*, of a body politic with the Prince as the head and animating force of other members were too literalist, too strongly corporatist, and too specifically Christian to serve the new order they were creating. But they were nonetheless haunted by Hebrew and Christian images of a covenanted polity: The body is one but has many members. There is, there can be, unity with diversity.

Indeed, one could even go so far as to insist that it is incorporation, enfolding within a single body, that makes meaningful diversity possible. Our differences must be recognized if they are to exist substantively at all. As political philosopher Charles Taylor writes, ". . . my discovering my own identity doesn't mean that I work it out in isolation, but that I negotiate it through dialogue, partly overt, partly internal, with others. . . . My own identity crucially depends on my dialogical relations with others." (Charles Taylor, *Multiculturalism and the Politics of Recognition*, Princeton University Press, 1992, p. 34.) What this means is that we cannot be different all by ourselves. A political body that brings people together, creating a "we," but that enables these same persons to separate themselves and to recognize one another in and through their differences as well as in what they share in common—that was the great challenge. It remains the great challenge.

Our World War I era forebears went too far in one direction—towards obliteration of difference itself. Our contemporaries, or many of the most quoted and vocal among us, go too far in another direction—towards obliteration of commonality and, indeed, occlusion of the notion of that bearer of the sign of our commonality—the citizen—altogether. The rhetoric of difference has supplanted the rhetoric of equality. But, oddly enough, it seems to be working towards its own homogenizing ends, at once hyperindividualistic and drearily conformist. Let me tell you a story from the conference front. I recall my shock at a conference I attended on women and feminism several years ago. For two and a half days, I listened to assaults on the very idea of democratic equality. Equality meant "the same." Equality was the mark of masculinism. Equality was the stigma of heterosexism. It was pretty much every nasty thing you could think of and come up with a name for. Somehow even the Nazis got to be perverse egalitarians in their rush to exterminate the different.

No, what women should be about, one attendee proclaimed, was implementing and celebrating their "will to power." Equality, that paltry thing, meant "homologization with the male subject." As that was news to me, I decided I needed to ponder this matter further. Recognizing that democracy without a notion of citizen equality is an impossible proposition, I got the uneasy feeling, one that remains with me to this day and has only been strengthened by recent celebrations of difference as a uniform and fixed group identity, that perhaps many of those immersed in militant versions of the "discourse of difference" are not so keen on constitutional democracy itself.

This is a worry. As George Kateb notes, "To want to believe that there is either a fixed majority interest or a homogeneous group identity is not compatible with the premises of rights-based individualism." (*The Inner*

Ocean, Cornell University Press, 1992, pp. 23–24.) Although I prefer to speak of democratic "individuality" rather than "individualism," Kateb's point seems to be well-taken. To the extent that citizens begin to retribalize into ethnic or other "fixed-identity groups," democracy falters. Any possibility for human dialogue, for democratic communication and commonality, vanishes as so much froth on the polluted sea of phony equality. Difference more and more becomes exclusivist. If you are black and I am white, by definition I do not and cannot, in principle, "get it." There is no way that we can negotiate the space between our pregiven differences. We are just stuck with them, stuck in what political theorists call "ascriptive characteristics"—things we cannot change about ourselves. Mired in the cement of our own identities, we need never deal with one another. We evade our citizen responsibilities. One of us will win, and one of us will lose the cultural war or the political struggle. That's what it's all about—power and nothing but power of the most impositional sort.

The political theorist Sheldon Wolin fears that the most important of all democratic categories—the citizen—will dissolve in the acids of this new ideology of difference, an ideology that despairs of, or huffily rejects, equality as "some broad measure of similarity if only to support a notion of membership that entails equality of rights, responsibilities, and treatment." ("Democracy, Difference, and Re-Cognition," *Political Theory,* Vol. 21, No. 3, August 1993, pp. 464–483, p. 466.) Repudiating the sameness of equality for its homogenizing urge, difference ideologues embrace their own version of sameness— an exclusionist sameness along lines of gender, race, ethnicity, and sexual preference. Ironically, it has traditionally been the "nondemocratic rulers, the men who justify their rule by appealing to differences—heredity, divinity, merit, knowledge—who reduce populations to a common condition," Wolin writes. (p. 476.)

Now others impatient with democratic principles, seeing in them little more than a cover for hidden privileges, demand public recognition for their own exclusivity. This leads to a terrible impasse, Wolin concludes, one to which "the politics of difference and the ideology of multiculturalism have contributed by rendering suspect the language and possibilities of collectivity, common action, and shared purposes." (p. 480.) Yet, at the same time, those pushing such a politics must, in practice, make appeal to "some culture of commonality" in launching their demands that their differences be respected and their grievances responded to. In other words, they disdain that on which they themselves depend for recognition.

It comes down to this: If you insist that what politics must consist in is my acknowledging and recognizing your difference, but at the same time, I am not allowed to engage you about this difference directly because we have nothing to say to one another, then I can only respond that you are not thinking and acting like a democratic citizen. You are thinking and acting like a royal pain in the neck and the sooner I can get you out of sight and mind, I will, not because I am a racist or a sexist or a homophobe or any of the other handy labels we toss around all too easily these days, but because I am weary of being accused of bad faith no matter what I do, or say, or refrain from doing or saying.

How did we get into this mess? How did so many among us get captured by a harsh vision of difference that negates what we might have in common, now or at some future point? Part of the explanation, of course, lies in frustration with the terrible problems that continue to beset American life. Part of the explanation lies in authentic anger at indignities and indecency. But I am most concerned, as a political philosopher, with that part of the explanation which rests squarely on a failure in the democratic imagination and a failure to pass on democratic verities. I am concerned with families and schools, as well as political institutions. I will focus on just one of these concerns—education—showing just how far we have fallen down in our responsibility to transmit democratic dispositions and faith in the possibilities of our central institutions.

Bear in mind the following: It was taken for granted from the start of the American democratic experiment that the survival of the republic for any length of time would depend heavily on cultivating civic sentiments among the young. The optimistic hope was that national character could itself be formed by careful molding of the children of each new generation. The indefatigable American Founders debated education, rejecting explicitly a classic civic republican education modeled on the example of ancient Sparta precisely because it demanded and likely yielded homogeneity and sameness. In Federalist Paper Number 10, Publius advances a commitment to civility that implies tolerance for difference, as well as political equality. The "spirit of the people," informed by religious principles and a belief in nature and nature's laws, required no fixed and dogmatic creed.

This version of difference involved awareness of different opinions: we don't all think alike. The claims to difference were made on an epistemological rather than an ontological level, by contrast to much contemporary multiculturalism with its vision of exclusivist groups given ontologically: This is what we *are*. This claim that there is such a thing as "thinking black" or "thinking white" is a way of thinking my parents taught me was racist when I was growing up in a little village in rural Colorado. But, according to this claim, you are one thing or another, you can't help it, and it determines everything about you. To the extent that educators put themselves at the service of this latter version of multiculturalism, they disastrously abandon the turf they were deeded, the space within which they were enjoined to help create a commitment to a rough-and-ready social egalitarianism coupled with an equally strong commitment to civility. But how can imposed uniformity—whether of sameness or difference—prepare citizens of a democracy to exercise civic and social responsibilities? The answer, of course, is that it cannot.

What, then, are our options? How do we recapture or, perhaps better put, struggle to sustain that peculiar democratic agon, the ongoing negotiation of difference and commonalities, of distinctiveness and equality? Not being simple, democracy does not afford us a straightforward definition of what education for citizenship in democratic responsibility might be. We are on the horns of more than one dilemma. But we must try to fix at least a few notions and meanings, for to abandon that attempt altogether would be to live in an amorphous and pointless world in which nobody cared very much about anything. Because a democratic culture is one in which responsibility and freedom go hand-in-hand, human beings, limited though they may be, can and must sort out the important from the less important, the vital from the trivial, the worthy from the unworthy, the excellent from the mediocre. Democracy is a culture of, and for, the stout-hearted, persons who, in their effort to define and to realize the good life, can live with a certain amount of uncertainty.

From Jefferson's bold throwing down of the gauntlet to the British Empire, not knowing whether the upshot would be hanging together or being hanged separately, to Lincoln's "nation thus conceived and thus dedicated," to Martin Luther King's dream of an essentially pacific democratic people who judge their fellow citizens by the content of their character, not the color of their skins, democratic culture has been a *wager*, not a frozen accomplishment. I mention these exemplars from the past in order to remind us that how we acknowledge and view the past forms a frame of reference for our understandings of the perils and possibilities of the present. We are entangled with and against tradition, and the democratic tradition is not of a piece. Indeed, human life itself, in any complex modern culture, especially our own, is an ongoing contestation over the meaning of tradition and the ways in which we would affirm or challenge that which is given to us in our particular time and place.

But in a world of overheated political demands, in a world in which rights alone are triumphant and responsibilities wither on the civic vine, we are in danger of losing the richness of democratic contestation. Consider the following examples. A class takes up the Declaration of Independence and the grand pronouncement that "All men are created equal." But women (and many men) were disenfranchised. Slaves were not even counted as full persons. How could this be, the teacher asks? What meaning of equality did the Founders embrace? Were any of them uneasy about this? How did they square this shared meaning of their own time with what we perceive to be a manifest set of injustices that precisely denied to many persons the dignity and responsibility of free citizenship? What got debated and what did not? What political and moral exigencies of that historic moment compelled what sorts of compromises? Might things have gone differently? And so on. This I take to be an instance of reflective political education about and for American democracy and our own perennial dilemma of the one and the many.

But let me put a second example. A teacher declares that nothing good ever came from the hand of that abstract, all-purpose villain, the "dead, white European male." The words and deeds of such men, including the Founders, are nefarious. They were nothing but racists and patriarchalists, blatant oppressors who hid behind fine-sounding words. All they created is tainted and hypocritical. There is no ambiguity. Here the matter simply ends. All is foreclosed. All has been exposed. The world closes in. Debate ends or is discouraged. To express a different point of view is to betray one's own false consciousness, venality, or white, patriarchal privilege. This I take to be an instance of unreflective, dogmatic politicization. It evades the dilemmas of democratic citizenship rather than offering us points of critical reflection on those dilemmas. This sort of education fails in its very particular and important task of preparing us for a world of rights with responsibilities, of ambiguities and settled meanings. It equips us only for resentment.

Our democratic culture is dependent on responsibility and self-limiting freedom. The danger in any ideological

definition of education is that it undermines, even negates, this essential dimension. We cede responsibility to
a Weltanschauung. Because democracy is the political
form that permits and requires human freedom as responsibility, any definition or system of education or
politics that sanctions evasion of responsibility imperils
democracy. (I draw here and above on portions of my
essay, "Democracy's Middle Way: An Essay on 'Can Education be Defined?'" *The World and I*, January 1993,
461–473.) Whether in the name of change or to forestall
all change, an ideological system of education or an ide-
ologically charged politics is the worst possible way for
human beings to order their collective affairs. For once a
world of personal responsibility with its characteristic
virtues and marks of decency (justice, honor, friendship,
fidelity) is ruptured or emptied, what rushes in to take
its place is politics as a "technology of power," in Václav
Havel's phrase. (See, especially, Havel's essay, "Power
and Powerlessness," in *Living in Truth*, Faber and
Faber, 1987.) Responsibility, according to Havel—and
he is as surefooted a guide as any currently available—
flows from the aims of life "in its essence," and these are
plurality and independent self-constitution as opposed to
the conformity, uniformity, and stultifying dogmas of
left- and right-wing ideologues who abandon reality and
assault life with their rigid, abstract chimeras.

In a way we are borne back to our understanding of the
democratic idiom itself and its characteristic categories
and meanings—freedom and responsibility and equality
being three of the most important. Such words are always open to contestation and redefinition. But there is a
limit to this process of redefinition. Words may, over
time, be denuded of meaning rather than enhanced by

definitional contestation without end. Part of our own culture's desperate floundering stems from the fact that we have lost any solidity to our understanding of the most basic things. Words have become rootless, homeless.

This has come about for some good reasons—recognition of the slipperiness of definitions, for example—but more and more, for some very bad reasons, too—such as cynicism bordering on vulgar antinomianism about the need for at least provisional (and no doubt imperfect) sharing of certain key words like freedom, responsibility, and equality. If we hold in unrelenting contempt any and all attempts to articulate the norms we *must* share in order that democratic debate and dialogue are ongoingly reaffirmed as the way we—citizens of a democratic culture—do business with one another, then we finally will not be able to do business with one another. We will set up the civic equivalent of tariff barriers and visas and categories of undesirable aliens.

Let me return to Václav Havel. A fusion of freedom and responsibility of the sort he embraces yields a distinct but definite political conclusion: Democracy is the political form that permits and requires human freedom, not as an act of self-overcoming or of pure reason, but in service to others in one's own time and place. To live "within the truth" is to give voice to a self that has embraced responsibility for the here and now. "That means that responsibility is ours, that we must accept it and grasp it *here, now,* in this place in time and space where the Lord has set us down, and that we cannot lie our way out of it by moving somewhere else, whether it be to an Indian ashram or a parallel polis," writes Havel. ("Power and Powerless," p. 104.)

Havel believes we are living in the midst of a general crisis of human consciousness. That crisis manifests itself in the spheres of human freedom, responsibility, and identity itself. Acceptance of the risks of free action makes one a person and forms the basis of one's identity. Any mode of thought or public policy or political agenda or program of education that reduces human responsibility narrows the horizon of human possibility. To assume "full responsibility" is not to lapse into dour moralism, not to universalize a giddy and boundless compassion, but to take up the specific, concrete burdens of one's own culture. Multiculturalism as an ideology of separatism and victimization undermines this possibility by offering us a world that is too simplistic—a world in which some are oppressors and some are oppressed, in which some are charged with violations and held accountable for every wrong, real or imagined, and others are not responsible for anything because they haven't held power.

This is precisely the vulgar view of the world Havel challenges. He has reminded his fellow Czechs again and again that they cannot blame all their woes on Communist oppressors; they, too, are responsible in particular ways for the terrible order of things that held their society in thrall for nearly half a century. Needless to say, this is not a message many of his colleagues and compatriots want to hear. It is not a message many Americans are prepared to credit at all, for it lets no one off the hook. Rather, it alerts us to the fact that we are in danger of forfeiting our cultural heritage because too many among us have convinced themselves that that heritage represents only the detritus of power and chicanery rather than the way imperfect human beings, only a few of whom were villains, have offered us the fruits of their strengths and their weaknesses, their moments of honor and their hours of despair.

Let me conclude these reflections by asking the reader to join me in a little village in the irrigated farm country of rural Colorado, a village named Timnath, pop. 185, where I grew up. For that is where my own democratic dreams were nurtured. The Timnath Public School, District Number 62, housed grades 1 through 12 in a single building: there weren't that many of us. I remember that we memorized the Declaration of Independence and the Gettysburg Address. The Gettysburg Address recitation, when my classmates and I reached Grades 7 and 8— one classroom under the firm if somewhat eccentric tutelage of Miss McCarthy—was always quite an event. We would line up in a single row around the classroom. On Miss McCarthy's signal, we would hum the "Battle Hymn of the Republic" as she recited the Gettysburg Address with flourish and fervor. She had a way of trailing off each sentence in a trembling, melodramatic whisper that left us hummers in stitches. But I never forgot the Gettysburg Address and its promise of democratic equality.

My democratic dream was nurtured by a presumption that we were not stuck inside our own skins, that our identities were not reducible to our membership in a race, an ethnic group, or a sex. I remember my father telling me that the "Mexican kids"—Mexican being the term of respect in that time and place—were sometimes smart and sometimes not, just like other kids. Before Martin Luther King made it the central theme of his great "I have a dream" speech, I had already learned that I was to judge others, not by the color of their skins but by the content of their character. It would never have occurred to me that I should "think girlishly" or that my friend, Raymond Barros, was required to "think with his blood."

By the time we reached high school in that isolated little place, our text for English class was called *Adventures in Reading*, published by Harcourt, Brace. I still have my copy, having purchased it from the school because I loved so many of the stories and poems it contained. The Table of Contents was divided into "Good Stories Old and New," with such gracing subsections as "Winning Against the Odds," "Meeting the Unusual," and "Facing Problems." We read "Lyrics from Many Lands" and "American Songs and Sketches." I looked at this text recently as I thought about multiculturalism, citizenship, democracy, and responsibility, as I thought about what I would write for this essay and how I would write it. By no means was this a text dominated by a single point of view, that of the dread dead white European male. We read Mary O'Hara, Dorothy Canfield, Margaret Weymouth Jackson, Elsie Singmaster, Selma Lagerlof, Rosemary Vincent Benet, Kathryn Forbes, Sarojini Naidu, Willa Cather, Emily Dickinson, on and on. We read the great abolitionist, Frederick Douglass, and the black reformer, Booker T. Washington. We read Leo Tolstoy and Pedro de Alarcon. We read translations of Native American warrior songs.

Now this reading wasn't done under the specific rubric of multiculturalism. But it was undertaken on the assumption that life is diverse, filled with many wonders. Through *Adventures in Reading*, we could make the lives and thoughts of others somehow, in some way, our own. In my imaginings and yearnings, I didn't feel constrained because some of those I most admired were men. I later chafed against constraints that lay outside my imagination, of course, but education is about opening the world up, not imprisoning us in terms of race, gender, or ethnicity. I was taught, "Reading is your passport to adventure in faraway places. In books the world lies before you, its paths radiating from great cities to distant lands, to scenes forever new, forever changing. . . . Reading knows no barrier, neither time nor space nor bounds of prejudice—it admits us all to the community of human experience." Clearly, I was a lucky child, a lucky democratic child. I had been invited into adventures in self-understanding that encouraged a broad perspective and a specific sense of responsibility—both, one and the same, enriching and enforcing one another.

This work of opening us up to a wide and wondrous world and helping us to frame the boundaries and terms of responsibility to and for it can be neither the exclusive purview of the family nor of some overweening state or bureaucracy, whether it is pushing homogeneity or multiculturalism. It is a task of civil society—of families, schools, voluntary associations, churches, a rich social ecology. A democratic culture is a porous affair, open to that wide world, but that does not mean it must needs become the plaything of purveyors of passing enthusiasms, whether political or pedagogical. The danger in continuing down our present path is that we are losing education in, to, and for self-limiting freedom—education in its widest sense, as the work of an entire culture.

Because democracy is the political form that permits and requires human freedom as responsibility, any definition or system that sanctions evasion of responsibility—as, say, I sink my identity totally into that of a group and its "group think"—imperils democracy. Democracy is for the stout of heart who know there are things worth fighting for in a world of paradox, ambiguity, and irony. This democratic way—moderation with courage, open to compromise from a basis of principle—is the rare but now and then attainable fruit of the democratic imagination and, in action, the responsible democratic citizen.

THE INDIVIDUAL'S SEARCH FOR TRUTH—
AND ITS LIMITATIONS

by

Jaroslav Pelikan

Jaroslav Pelikan

Jaroslav Pelikan is Sterling Professor of History at Yale University, where he has taught since 1962. At Yale he was Titus Street Professor from 1962 to 1972, Dean of the Graduate School from 1973 to 1978, and William Clyde DeVane Lecturer from 1984 to 1986. He was educated at Concordia (Junior College) in Fort Wayne, Indiana; Concordia Theological Seminary in St. Louis, Missouri; and The University of Chicago. Before coming to Yale, he taught at Valparaiso University, Concordia Theological Seminary, and The University of Chicago.

Among the thirty books Professor Pelikan has written are From Luther to Kierkegaard *(1950),* The Christian Intellectual *(1966),* The Christian Tradition *(in five volumes, 1971–1989),* Scholarship and Its Survival *(1983),* The Vindication of Tradition *(1984),* Jesus through the Centuries *(1985),* Eternal Feminines *(1990),* The Idea of the University—A Reexamination *(1992), and* Christianity and Classical Culture *(1993). He has also served as editor for many books including* Luther's Works *(in 22 volumes, 1955–1971) and* Twentieth-Century Theology in the Making *(in three volumes, 1969–1970).*

Professor Pelikan has received honorary degrees from thirty-five colleges and universities. He is President-Elect of the National Academy of Arts and Sciences.

THE INDIVIDUAL'S SEARCH FOR TRUTH—
AND ITS LIMITATIONS

by

Jaroslav Pelikan

The overall theme of the Andrew R. Cecil Lectures for 1993 is "Individualism and Social Responsibility." Within this series my specific assignment, as Dr. Andrew R. Cecil formulated it in his letter of invitation to me dated April 6, 1993, is "to address the topic of the university's role in developing individualism and preparing students to discharge their social responsibilities." Both of the key concepts in the theme of the Lectureship, "individualism" and "social responsibility," are subtle and profound in their implications and call for careful definition, especially in the form in which they are involved in the research and the teaching that together constitute the mission of the university.

The primary business of the university is knowledge. For any definition of "individualism" in the role of the university, as it affects this or any other aspect of its mission, therefore, the fundamental charter was formulated by Aristotle (whom Dante called "master of those who know"), in the opening words of his *Meta-physics* (980a21-27):

> "All men by nature desire to know. An indication of this is the delight we take in our senses; for even apart from their usefulness they are loved for themselves; and above all others the sense of sight. For not only with a view to action, but even when

215

we are not going to do anything, we prefer sight to
almost everything else. The reason is that this,
most of all the senses, makes us know and brings to
light many differences between things."

But the same Aristotle is also the author of what has
probably been the most influential definition ever provided for our other key term, "social responsibility," as
he formulated this in another of his major philosophical
treatises, this time in the *Politics*, but once again in the
first book (1253al–10):

"Hence it is evident that the state is a creation of
nature, and that man is by nature a political
animal [or, perhaps a better translation: a social
being, as a member of the *polis*]. And he who by
nature and not by mere accident is without a state,
is either a bad man or above humanity. . . . Now,
that man is more of a political animal [social being]
than bees or any other gregarious animals is
evident. Nature, as we often say, makes nothing in
vain, and man is the only animal whom she has
endowed with the gift of speech."

My assignment in this lecture series, of relating "the
development of individualism" to "the discharge of social
responsibility," and of doing so in the context of "the role
of the university," consequently, may in a sense be said to
be one of correlating the dynamics set forth in these two
Aristotelian definitions. Both of them, it should be noted,
invoke as the standard of judgment a normative understanding of what humanity is "by nature [*physei*]," a concept that Aristotle cites in each definition. "Nature

[*physis*]" is for Aristotle a fundamental metaphysical category, which he defines in the *Physics* (192b23–25) as "a source or cause of being moved and of being at rest in that to which it properly belongs, in virtue of itself and not in virtue of a concomitant attribute." As Werner Jaeger has pointed out in his magisterial study, *Aristotle: Fundamentals of the History of His Development*, which was published in English translation in 1948, "it is a characteristically Aristotelian view that nature is purposive in a higher degree even than art, and that the purposiveness that rules in handiwork, whether art or craft, is nothing but an imitation of the purposiveness of nature" (p. 74). Thus the theme assigned to me for this lecture could be elaborated so as to read: What, within the mission of the university, is the relation to the development of the individual's "desire to know," which is "by nature," to the discharge of that individual's "social responsibility" as a "social being," which is also "by nature"?

I

One of the most important values that we as scholars strive both to exemplify in our own research and to transmit to the next generation of students in our teaching is the relentless search for truth, in accordance with Aristotle's axiom that "all men by nature desire to know." In his recent book, *Aristotle: The Desire to Understand* (Cambridge, 1988, p. 14), my Yale colleague Jonathan Lear has made this sage observation about that axiom:

> "Aristotle believed that to understand ourselves we must understand the world. He also believed

that to understand the world one must understand oneself. In particular, one cannot understand the world if one remains ignorant of the role the desire to understand plays in one's own soul as well as in the world at large, if one remains ignorant of the human mind and its capacity to understand, if one remains ignorant of the cost to oneself and to others of pursuing one's desire. Aristotle tried to raise himself and his students out of this ignorance. Though the modern world may have left the details of his account behind, his insistence that understanding and self-understanding are each dependent on the other is, I believe, a truth whose depth we have only begun to appreciate."

Professor Lear's observation about the need to appreciate the depth of Aristotle's insistence upon the interdependence between understanding and self-understanding, as that need has been brought home to twentieth-century thought, is especially pertinent to our theme here. For it is precisely at the point of that interdependence that the development of individualism and the discharge of social responsibility can collide most easily and, conversely, at the point of that interdependence that their fundamental compatibility must become clear and explicit in the life of the university and in the intellectual and moral formation of its students as the university prepares them, through addressing their desire to know, for responsible participation in the future as social and political beings.

Although all of this has always been true, in a variety of times and through a succession of cultures, our own time is witnessing a deepening disaffection with higher

education and a growth in what I have elsewhere called
"university-bashing." Much of this criticism of the university, moreover, is focused on university research, and
above all on the sort of basic research that does not trans-
late into immediate social or economic results, which is
the kind of research that university scholars prize highly
but that (to put it mildly) many others do not appreciate
equally. The single-minded search for truth by the individual scholar or scientist, irrespective of the consequences, thus becomes, in the eyes of such critics, the
ultimate form of self-indulgence, which is made all the
worse because it is being subsidized by the well-meaning
but ill-informed taxpayers or being shielded from
reality and from responsibility and accountability by the
university's endowment. The students, meanwhile, who
have naively come to the university because they want to
learn (as Aristotle said they should), become the victims
of their professors' self-indulgence and must be content
with being taught chiefly by graduate assistants.

As I have recently suggested elsewhere, it would be intriguing for a scholar in American Studies to write a
comparative history of the relative standing of the
several professions in American public opinion over the
past century or so: the clergy, the law, medicine, and
business have all experienced rises and falls in esteem,
as scandals and successes have cast their reflections or
shadows on the profession. In those rises and falls, the
profession of the scholar and scientist has passed
through its own version of this development. At present,
it seems to me, it stands under a considerable shadow,
and it would appear that now it has come to be our turn to
go through what Sinclair Lewis's *Elmer Gantry* meant
for the clergy or what Watergate did to the lawyers. The

phenomenon that I have called "university-bashing" makes itself visible in the seemingly ceaseless appearance of books and articles accusing the universities of price-gouging because the price of college tuition has been going up much faster than has the general cost of living. Especially inviting as a target for such exposés is university research. Because so much of the research that is done at American universities in the sciences receives its principal support from the federal government, through such agencies as the National Institutes of Health, political candidates and investigative reporters looking for instances of waste (or sometimes just for a "cheap shot") can focus in on the research laboratories that concentrate on the basic science which stands behind the applied research of medicine and pharmacology. The implication of such investigations is that millions of tax dollars have been going into investigations of rats or of enzymes from which no direct or immediate results can come for the cure of cancer, for the reduction of pollution, or for any other social good. In addition there has been, since Mary Wollstonecraft Shelley's *Frankenstein* of 1818 and even before, an entire literary genre, a subset of science fiction, describing the work of the "mad scientist," whose individualistic search for truth at any price brings on disastrous social and moral consequences. Although it is clear from his various novels related to this theme, from *The Andromeda Strain* to *Jurassic Park*, that Michael Crichton, with his own training in the biomedical sciences, has striven to avoid such clichés, some geneticists have been expressing the concern, especially in the aftermath of *Jurassic Park*, as a novel and now as a film, that the nervousness of the lay public about the potential consequences of

DNA research and of "genetic engineering" could lead to restrictions on their laboratories and to serious reductions in the levels of public and private support for such research.

Public attitudes toward basic research in the humanities and the social sciences are no less critical and no less dangerous, as some of the controversy surrounding the National Endowment for the Humanities and the National Endowment for the Arts has shown. For here the public interest in the outcomes of research leads to a sense of disappointment, or even of betrayal, if scholarly research and publication does not produce a deeper appreciation of a favorite poem or a more positive attitude toward the market economy and American society. The widespread—and, in its own context, understandable and justifiable—critique of the emphasis on humanistic research at the university because of its supposedly deleterious effect on undergraduate teaching frequently takes the form of charging that professors are individualistically paying attention to their "own work" (a locution by which somehow we always seem to be referring to our research and writing rather than to our teaching, almost as though this were being thought of as somebody else's work), at the expense of the classroom and its students. Scholarship in the humanities is seen as a not so subtle form of self-aggrandizement, and the system of incentives and rewards held out to university faculty seems to manifest far too pronounced an emphasis on research and publication, for all the lip service that is always paid to teaching. As Page Smith has suggested in his deeply felt polemic, *Killing the Spirit*, such research and publication may receive high praise and may earn academic promotion despite a banality and triviality that ought to be a fatal mark against it. All of us have experienced something of this sense, at any rate about research outside our own field of concentration, while sitting through an academic commencement, where the titles of the dissertations for which graduate students are receiving their Ph.D.s seem to be proof that all the significant research on Shakespeare or Plato has already been done, so that there is room only for the next generation of gleaners to search for tiny individual grains after the harvest is over. Meanwhile, it seems to many observers that the sense of social responsibility, which ought to be the mark of the scholar and teacher, is being overshadowed by this individualistic search for "truth," but for a "truth" that seems to come in ever smaller and smaller packages. What makes the whole system even worse, according to its critics, is that university students who are growing to maturity in such a setting will be led to believe that genuine scholarship does consist in these "trivial pursuits" and will go on individualistically perpetuating the set of values that they have learned from their university professors without paying sufficient attention to discharging their social responsibilities; alternately, they will be disaffected with the intellectual and scholarly life altogether.

As I suppose I have a right to assert on the basis of my own publications in the field of higher education, I am deeply aware of the crisis in the universities. I am no less deeply convinced, moreover, that the crisis is not merely political, as some of its observers seem to suppose, nor merely intellectual, as some of us (including myself) may sometimes have been inclined to conclude, but ultimately moral. It is a moral crisis because the relation between individualism and social responsibility, which it exemplifies and which this entire series of Andrew R. Cecil Lectures for 1993 on "Individualism and Social Responsibility" is intended to explore, is finally a moral issue. Our society, indeed every modern society, has an enormous financial and psychic stake in its universities, which are preparing for the future both in the classroom and in the laboratory and library. We who have been the beneficiaries of the universities founded by previous generations and of the instruction and example of our mentors have the obligation, both as scholars and as teachers, to address this moral dimension of our work. For, in my favorite epigram from Goethe's *Faust* (lines 682-683), a work to which I shall be returning at the conclusion of this lecture for its contribution to our overall theme,

> "What you have as heritage,
> Now take as task,
> For thus you will make it your own."

As members of the university and as citizens, we shall prove to have been unworthy recipients of that heritage unless we take on this task, and unless we do so while there is still time.

II

The right place to begin any such reconsideration is with the recognition that the individual's search for truth is itself an *ethical* imperative. Now it bears repeating and elaborating that such a search for truth is in addition both a practical and an aesthetic imperative. No amount of dedication to the ideal of "Knowledge Its Own End," the title that John Henry Cardinal Newman on the basis of Cicero gave to Discourse V of his book *The Idea of a University* and that I have given to Chapter 4 of my book *The Idea of the University—A Reexamination*, ought to be permitted to belittle the very pragmatic motivation that underlies much of the research that goes on. In some fields of the arts and sciences, of course, that motivation may perhaps be less visible than it is in various of the professions such as engineering, where, for example, the needs of the manufacturer for a better and safer product or for more efficient means of production are the direct reason for the research. University scholars sometimes tend to forget the vast amount of research, for example, in chemistry—and that does not mean only chemical engineering—that is being carried on under industrial auspices rather than under either academic or governmental auspices. A large percentage of the holders of the Ph.D. degree in chemistry—fully half, by some counts—can be found in the employ of industrial corporations and are in some way making a contribution to the manufactured products and the manufacturing processes of those corporations. Scholars in jurisprudence may sometimes seem to be ranging quite far afield in their studies, but it seems safe to say that most research by most legal scholars has as its purpose and as its result some concrete aspect of the practice of the law. But also in the arts and sciences, research aimed at the production of practical results is neither rare nor unworthy of praise. Having devoted a substantial portion of my own scholarly career to the editing and translating of texts in various languages, I know the sort of work that is involved in applying the methods of textual criticism in order to determine the most reliable reading of some older or newer writing, in probing the history of a word in Greek or Latin or German in order to determine what it might mean in this particular context, in tracking down allusions and quotations and identifying the sources upon which a writer drew whether consciously or unconsciously, and, finally, in rendering the results in an English that is simultaneously accurate and graceful. I have always insisted, moreover, that, aimed though it is at the extremely pragmatic results of an edition and translation, even an edition and translation for the general reader, such research can be among the most distinguished (and difficult) in the humanities.

In my address for the Sesquicentennial of Tulane University in 1984 on "The Aesthetics of Scholarly Research," I urged that there is also a dimension in scholarly research that must be identified as artistic. I mentioned there how struck I have been by the frequency with which the word "elegant," an aesthetic criterion, is used by professionals in the field to describe an experiment in medicine and science. The identification of a question for scholarly inquiry has much in common with the choice of a theme for artistic expression, because both are directed by some guiding vision. In the execution of the research, likewise, this aesthetic dimension is fundamental, because central elements in it are the same eye for the telling detail and the very sense of selectivity that are also manifest in the work of a great artist. Conversely, in aesthetic creativity no less than in scholarly investigation, there will always be a substantial amount of drudgery, what the Germans, with their long experience of scholarly research and their infallible instinct for the right word, call *Eselarbeit*. When undergraduates come to me to express an interest in going into the scholarly life, I enthusiastically welcome their interest; but eventually I get around to asking them: Are you really prepared to take on this *Eselarbeit*, and the loneliness and frustration that are its inevitable accompaniment? "To be a scholar," one of the greatest of them, Adolf von Harnack of the University of Berlin used to say, "it is necessary to be part monk—and to get an early start!" Above all, however, the aesthetics of scholarly research is, or at any rate should be, visible in its presentation. I keep insisting to all who are willing to listen that we who serve as graduate advisers and directors must not feel we have done our job until and unless we have communicated, both by precept and by example, the obligation to express the outcome of our research clearly and well.

Nevertheless, neither the pragmatic nor the aesthetic qualities of the search for truth are the most fundamental, for that search is ultimately an expression of ethical values. Having written various discourses, inspired by Aristotle and Cardinal Newman, on the "intellectual virtues," I shall not repeat myself here. Let me rather go on from those discourses of mine to enumerate, almost in the form of theses, some of the most important of the ethical values involved in that search.

1. The distinction between means and ends in such a search, which underlies Newman's chapter "Knowledge Its Own End," is itself a moral distinction. To quote again from Jaeger's *Aristotle* (p. 75), "Everything comes into being for the sake of an end. An end is that which always appears as the final result of a development, in accordance with natural law and by a continuous process, and in which the process attains its completion."

From what I have already said, it should, I hope, be clear that I do not dismiss as immoral or unimportant the use of knowledge as a means to another, more practical end. For such a use of knowledge, the morality consists primarily in the end being pursued, to which the knowledge serves as a means. If that end be moral, the search for knowledge in order to attain to it is also, at least in principle, moral (though not without some very important qualifications, to which I shall be turning a little later). Yet there remains a distinction between this search for knowledge as means and the search for knowledge as an end in itself, and one implication of the distinction is that the search for knowledge as an end in itself must find its moral justification within itself. It is intriguing in this connection to ponder the relation between two formulas that stand at the headwaters of our entire Western tradition, both the intellectual tradition and the ethical tradition: the axiom from Aristotle's *Metaphysics* that I quoted near the beginning of this lecture, "All men by nature desire to know," and the words of the serpent to Eve in the Genesis narrative of the Fall, "You will be like God, knowing good and evil" (Gen. 3:5, New Revised Standard Version). Ever since the Hellenistic Judaism of Philo of Alexandria, those who have stood simultaneously in the Greek tradition and in the biblical tradition have striven to find some kind of reconciliation between these two apparently contradictory approaches to knowing. This reconciliation has usually consisted in the argument, which seems to me to be sound, that if the innate desire to know of which Aristotle speaks is indeed "by nature" and is therefore a gift of the Creator, the "knowledge of good and evil" of which Genesis speaks as a great danger must in principle be something quite different from that desire, namely, a "knowledge" that includes the participation in evil and sin as well as in good, rather than the recognition of both good and evil for what they are, and that therefore represents the tempter's seduction and the tempter's curse. In this interpretation, the New Testament promise, "You will know the truth, and the truth sill make you free" (John 8:32, NRSV), has been taken as proof that the individual's search for truth is indeed God-given and God-pleasing. According to the best of the Jewish and Christian traditions, reflected for example in the address of the apostle Paul on the Areopagus in Athens (Acts 17:27), moreover, the search for truth is God-given and God-pleasing wherever it may have appeared in human life, not only in the true believer; it is, to invoke a distinction of Thomas Aquinas derived in part from Aristotle, "by nature" and not exclusively "by grace." That is likewise what I mean by calling it a moral imperative in itself.

2. From this primary moral imperative there flows as a necessary corollary the obligation on the part of the individual to acquire and polish the skills that are necessary to the search for knowledge, and thus to actualize to the fullest the potential that is there, which is what the Greeks meant by "excelling [aristeuein]" and by "excellence as virtue [aretē]." To quote again from Aristotle, this time from the *Nicomachean Ethics* (1177a12-14), "If happiness is activity in accordance with excellence as virtue, it is reasonable that it should be in accordance with the highest excellence as virtue; and this will be that of the best thing in us." Thus when John Milton, in his sonnet "On His Blindness," spoke of

" . . . that one Talent which is death to hide,
Lodg'd with me useless, though my Soul more bent
To serve therewith my Maker, and present
My true account, lest He returning chide;"

And when Gerard Manley Hopkins, in his poem "Morning Midday and Evening Sacrifice," exclaimed,

"This pride of prime's enjoyment
Take as for tool, not toy meant
And hold at Christ's employment—"

both of them, the first as a Puritan moralist and the second as a Jesuit moralist, were urging this obligation on their readers. Still, it is the universal experience of humanity that not all individuals possess the same capacity for such skills; nor do they possess these skills in the same measure. That universal experience, however, runs in the face of the egalitarian views so beloved of populist writers and politicians. It is amusing to note that even and especially in America everyone will freely acknowledge fundamental and innate differences between individuals when it comes to athletic skills, and will also concede to each individual the right and the duty to make the most of these skills even if they have obviously been distributed very unevenly across the populace. Yet just because I cannot run a four-minute mile does not imply that you should decline to do so if you are able, in order to spare my feelings. Why is it, then, that we tend to adopt such a different posture with regard to intellectual endowments and the palpable unevenness in the distribution of these endowments among various individuals? Whatever the psychological and historical answers to that question may be, as they relate to the endemic anti-intellectualism of America so graphically described by Richard Hofstadter in his Pulitzer Prize-winning book of 1964 on the subject, *Anti-Intellectualism in American Life,* the principal issue for my purposes here is the need to find and to articulate the moral nexus between natural endowment and acquired skill as this pertains to the life of the mind and to the individual's search for truth. If this be elitism, we may as well make the most of it! For where the capacity for intellectual achievement does manifest itself, it brings with it—in the life of the mind, no less than it does in athletics or in music—the moral obligation to develop it to the fullest extent possible.

3. But if I as an individual, as well as other individuals, do have that moral obligation, this entails, as another moral obligation, the need to monitor myself and others and to preserve intellectual honesty. Whether the phenomenon of scientific fraud and scholarly plagiarism is actually on the increase in our own time or not—and the impressions and opinions on this question vary, even among informed observers—every scholar would have to admit in moments of utter frankness to having at least been tempted to take a scholarly shortcut at one time or another. Therefore every scholar will (or should) also admit the need both for self-monitoring and for systematic monitoring within the entire scholarly profession on a field-by-field basis. To be sure, the potential for abuse in such a system of monitoring is great, and it is easy to cross the line from professional scrutiny into the competitive belittlement of colleagues and of their achievements. We have all read (or have perhaps even perpetrated) book reviews that have crossed this line; some of

the choicest tidbits of these have been collected in the
wickedly funny little book, *Rotten Reviews: A Literary
Companion,* edited by Bill Henderson in 1986. That is
why the moral case for this practice must begin with
what Jonathan Lear calls Aristotle's "insistence that
understanding and self-understanding are each dependent on the other," which is, he continues, "a truth whose
depth we have only begun to appreciate." The beginning
of wisdom here is the radical kind of moral self-understanding that F. M. Dostoevsky, who analyzed the
psychology of the murderer Raskolnikov with such
devastating penetration in *Crime and Punishment,*
expressed when he said that there was no crime of which
he knew himself to be incapable.

4. On the positive side, the moral imperative for the
individual to search for truth leads to the recognition
that no one can discharge such an obligation casually or
quickly. Rather, the term "obligation" must give way
here to something even more committed and sustained,
for which a more satisfactory term would probably be
"vocation." Just as the individual does not exist in isolation but must find self-expression and self-understanding in a social context, so a truth pursued by that
individual does not exist in isolation but is connected to
other truths—and to other people's truths. That is why
religious and cultural traditions as widely separated
from one another as the Buddhist, the Jewish, the Greek,
and the Christian have all developed this conception of
the search for truth as a vocation, and why our own
understanding of it carries so many of the same connotations, including the recognition that nothing less than an
entire lifetime is the appropriate measure for such a
vocation. Speaking at least for myself, I have often said

that if I had inherited or married great wealth, I would have wanted to devote my lifetime to scholarship just as I have done. For this, too, is part of the moral duty laid upon any individual who undertakes such a search: to stay with it relentlessly, and not to be willing to surrender it when professional or financial success may make it seem that it is no longer necessary, because the quest for such success was not the motivation of the search in the first place.

5. It also belongs to the moral imperative of the individual's relentless and lifelong pursuit of truth through research that such an individual assume the responsibility of sharing the results of that research with others. Thus "Publish or perish," which critics of the system of faculty appointment in the university so frequently cite as evidence of its inherent injustice when a favorite teacher of undergraduates fails to be promoted to tenure, is in fact an essential component of its ethic. Like the apostles in the New Testament (Acts 4:20, NRSV), "we cannot keep from speaking about what we have seen and heard," about those things to which our research investigations have led us. The moral foundation of this imperative is at least twofold. On the one hand, as that quotation from the Book of Acts suggests, there is a necessary correlation between the drive to pursue the truth and the drive to share it, a correlation that finds expression both through the classroom activity of the scholar-as-teacher and through the publications of the scholar-as-author. Without engaging in any romanticism about the "thrill of discovery," it would seem fair to suggest that the same form of intellectual excitement that inspired the original investigation will go on to impel the investigator to publish the results of the in-

vestigation. And on the other hand, what I called earlier "the moral obligation to monitor myself and others" implies that the individual should share the results of research also in order to give others the opportunity to replicate the research and to corroborate or, if necessary, to correct the results. Footnotes, those ofttimes ridiculed artifacts of the scholarly publication (which the German classicist Ulrich von Wilamowitz-Moellendorff once called globs of fat floating on the philological soup), are in fact an epitome of this moral principle. Anyone who wishes—and, to pick up on an earlier point, who has taken the trouble to acquire the necessary technical skills and scholarly credentials to handle the assignment—may verify my results by checking them against the sources. In addition, the footnote is the best device invented so far to acknowledge, in specific detail and not only in a general tribute, the scholar's debt to earlier scholars and, conversely, to define with some precision whatever divergence from them further investigation may require; as I shall suggest in greater detail a little later, both the acknowledgment of debt and the candid recognition of divergence also belong to the moral imperative of scholarship.

III

Stated as I have just stated it, this formulation of the moral grounds for the individual's search for knowledge has traditionally constituted the ethos of scholarly research. The biographies and autobiographies of scientists and scholars, together with the tributes to them by their own students in volumes dedicated to their honor or to their memory, have transmitted these warnings and exhortations from one generation to the next, through the description of scholarly role models and through the accumulation of academic folklore or gossip. Considerably less frequent and less explicit in the literature has been the identification of the various kinds of limitations to which the individual's search for knowledge is subject, and therefore of the social responsibilities an individual incurs in taking on such a search. Or, to put it in the Aristotelian framework with which I began, "the desire to know," which all individuals have "by nature," needs to find its context and its fulfillment in the social responsibilities of those individuals, because they are "social beings," and are so likewise "by nature." To individuals in their twenties, who are beginning to get a sense of their own intellectual powers and who are just learning the excitement of being able to stretch them, it is not easy to speak about "limitations" of this or of any other kind. As many of us have reason to remember, this can be a time when a young scholar feels capable of accomplishing practically anything. Yet the moral case undergirding the search for truth is not only deficient without a consideration of these limitations; it is morally dangerous and socially irresponsible.

Some of the limitations lie in the very nature of things and may be said to be intrinsic. Those "individuals in their twenties, who are beginning to get a sense of their own intellectual powers and who are just learning the excitement of being able to stretch them" of whom I spoke will, alas, not be in their twenties very long. The Latin proverb, "*vita brevis, ars longa* [life is short, but art is enduring]," is not only a celebration of the permanent value of the artistic and intellectual creations of the human mind and spirit; it is also a reminder that although the work of art may remain, the artist will not. An essential implication of this sobering reminder is that no search for truth, regardless of how single-minded the individual may be about it, can break out of these intrinsic limitations. Anyone who has undertaken, as I did when my scholarly life began more than fifty years ago, to carry out a major investigation that will require decades (in my case, four decades) of research and that will need several volumes (in my case, five volumes) to convey the results must do so with an acute sense of these limitations. It requires very fortunate timing, what the Greeks called a sense of *kairos*, to decide when the investigation has been going on long enough to warrant a commitment to begin the actual writing; starting too soon or waiting too long can be equally disastrous. In all of this, moreover, the individual takes on such a commitment with no guarantees. The history of scholarship—and, as we all know from our browsings, the shelves of research libraries— are littered with the torsos of partially completed works that, Ozymandias-like, stand there to warn future generations of scholars to respect above all the limitation imposed by their own mortality: "Look on my works, ye mighty, and despair!" Yet the recognition of this limitation must not be permitted to transform the search for truth into its caricature, which is all too familiar especially in the academy, the cautious preoccupation with presumably manageable investigations that add to information without increasing knowledge. In addition to the other evils it brings, this caricature provides the university-bashers of whom I spoke earlier with more ammunition than they deserve to have.

Another form of limitation on the individual's search

for truth, and one more closely related to the question of
social responsibility, is the limitation imposed on the
individual by various social institutions and economic
realities. In many fields of investigation, particularly in
the natural sciences, the inexorable realities of research
support and outside funding may quite effectively define
the limits of the research. Nor do those limits affect only
the work of senior scholars and principal investigators.
Because grant support for research has also become the
principal mechanism for funding graduate study in
many branches of the sciences and thus for preparing
the next generation of investigators, the choices for
graduate students may often be quite severely limited by
such grant support. Sometimes as a result of this situation, but more generally as a result of what previous
generations of scholars and administrators have or have
not done, the research both of senior and of junior scholars is limited also by the availability of the means and
tools for carrying it out within the facilities of any one
institution. As a graduate professor and especially
during my five years as a graduate school dean, I have
often pondered the problem of training graduate students from the Third World in the atmosphere of the
Yale laboratories and their instruments, or of the Yale
libraries, backed up as they are by the support system of
on-line catalogs, CD-ROMs, interlibrary loans, and relatively easy access to great collections, only to send them
back into a setting where, having become accustomed to
this style of research, they will face major frustration.
The irony of that predicament is often accentuated by
the circumstance that the accumulation of the primary
data for such research, whether in the form of manu-
script study or of anthropological observation, must

often take place precisely where these limitations are the most pronounced. There are very few scholarly obligations more pressing for the next generation than this, to make the search for truth truly international by easing the access to the needed resources and by developing a usable scholarly technology to bridge this gap. Yet the limitations are there, and some of them will remain, and not only in the Third World. The gravity of the problem is complicated still further by the political limitations that are placed on the individual's search for truth— often, indeed in the name of "social responsibility."

Both of these sets of limitations on the individual's search for knowledge can constitute major problems. But for my purposes in the present setting the most important limitations are not those imposed from outside the individual, either by institutions or even by human mortality, but those which the individual must learn to assume from within, as part of the obligation to carry on the search for truth within the limitations of social and moral responsibility—if you will, those that are not dependent on social, political, and economic pressure, but that are rather derived from conscience and from "the moral law within." Having earlier defined five principles about the ethical values involved in the individual's search for truth, let me match them with five rather loosely connected observations about the ethical limitations through which the individual learns to recognize the meaning of social responsibility. The first of them is a general moral principle, indeed, I believe, a universal principle, which has been brought home to our own century by its unique experiences with the reality of demonic power; the others, while grounded in such principles and experiences, have a special pertinence to the realm of thought and scholarship.

1. Inevitably, I come to the consideration of these
issues as a scholar whose special field of research and
writing is the history of Christian doctrine, which was
created and developed by German professors of theology
as *Dogmengeschichte*, and also as the author of *The Idea of
the University—A Reexamination*, which may in many
significant ways be characterized as a defense and elab-
oration of the culture of the German university, where
research and teaching are inseparably linked in the job
description of the university professor. As it has done for
many other scholars who belong to my generation, therefore, the traumatic experience of the German university
and of German scholarship during the twentieth century
has seriously colored and defined my approach, compelling me to qualify and to reformulate what I mean by
the individual's search for truth. Let me put this polem-
ical issue just as directly as possible. Was there, we are
morally compelled to ask, a necessary and logical connection between the dedication of German scholarship to
research and to the relentless search for truth at any
price, what has sometimes been called its *Forschertitan-
ismus*, and the willingness of some scholars and scientists during the Nazi era to resort to torture and to
chemical manipulation as means of extracting that truth
from unwilling human subjects? And conversely, does
that nightmare of the "Nazi doctors" have something
fundamental to tell us about the limitations that social
and moral responsibility places upon the individual's
search for truth? I am profoundly convinced that it does
have something to tell us, something to which we had
better listen. As it happens, the most powerful formulation of the moral principle at stake in this question has

also come from the German intellectual tradition, in this instance from Immanuel Kant's doctrine of the categorical imperative and of the "kingdom of ends." We must act in such a way, Kant warned, that we always regard a fellow human being as an end, not as a means to some other end; as he said, "respect applies always to persons only—not to things." For exploitation is the opposite of that principle, the willingness to sacrifice the worth of another human being to some lesser end. Both in the Judaeo-Christian tradition and in the tradition of Greek idealism especially as systematized by Plato—and thus in the philosophy of Kant, which is, in this and in other respects, a reflection of that combination of traditions—this principle is derived from the doctrine of the image of God: Because that is the unique privilege of humanity, a human being bears both a special responsibility and a special authority in relation to other beings, which are not endowed with the image. It is, then, humanity as a participant in the image of God that must, according to Kant, be treated as an end, not as a means. In that context, "exploitation" can be said to consist in violating the image of God by subordinating and manipulating human beings as though they were less than human. But even apart from the Judaeo-Christian doctrine of creation in the image of God, I would argue, the case of the Nazi doctors must serve as a major cautionary tale for an understanding of how to correlate the individual's search for truth with that same individual's discharge of social responsibilities.

2. While that warning from Kant about means and ends pertains with equal force to a full range of these social responsibilities, from the family to the workplace, there are also certain moral considerations that apply

with special force to scholarship and to the individual's search for truth. One of the most vexing of these is based on the entire ambiguous relation between the search for truth and the proposal of a hypothesis, and therefore pertains to the relation between hypothesis and fraud. As I have made clear earlier, I do not believe that there is any reliable methodology for determining whether the incidence of fraud among scholars and scientists has been increasing in recent years or not. Many serious observers are persuaded that there has not been any such increase, but only an increased sensitivity to the problem within the scientific and general communities, as well as a corresponding upsurge of curiosity about it also in the media. But quite apart from that question, there remains the moral problem of the proper place of hypothesis in the individual's search for truth. It is a problem that dogs this search at each stage. For contrary to the abstract version of it that can be found in books on scholarly or scientific method as well as in some autobiographies, the very selection of a topic for investigation already represents a mental tilt in the direction of a hypothesis: Why dig here rather than there unless there is already such a tilt? As the investigation progresses, it produces a revision of the original question. This can perhaps even lead to a surrender of the search altogether. More often, however, as the investigation progresses and as the topic of the inquiry is revised and sharpened, this represents in fact at least a preliminary sense of where the research is leading—whether or not that is the hunch from which the investigation took its original impulse. Once this preliminary sense arrives, how much more evidence is necessary to confirm the hypothesis? Clearly, one of the direct moral implications of the search for truth is that the investigator must above all give serious consideration to the evidence that seems to contradict the working hypothesis. But a simple-minded pettifoggery about this stage of the investigative process will tend to concentrate on this moral implication, to the exclusion of the no less compelling moral obligation to take some intellectual risks. The old motto of the sailor, "Risk nothing and do nothing," applies no less to the scholar, and this is no less a social obligation, because in some instances the discovery of truth and even the welfare of society may well depend more upon creative risks than upon caution. It is probably fair to say that as an adviser and mentor of graduate students, I have more often had to push them toward such risks than to restrain them from reckless speculation and premature formulation of hypotheses. But there have been just enough cases of the opposite problem to warrant our paying careful attention to both sides of this polarity.

3. An intriguing moral problem in the search for truth is the ethics of acknowledgments, to which I have alluded earlier. Many scholarly books will contain a special section in the front matter for acknowledgments; when these manage to get beyond the cliche of "without whom this book would never have been written" (whether that be true or not), such acknowledgments can be, in both intellectual and moral terms, an important device for preserving honesty and integrity in scholarship. So subtle and complex is the interaction between teacher and student, between colleague and colleague, between the history of a discipline and its present practice, that an author should look for ways to chart the pedigree of an idea to which, now, this book or article is giving more or less definitive formulation. Thus I have sometimes had

the experience of throwing out a suggestion as an *obiter dictum* in a seminar or a lecture, then of having it picked up by one of my students who proceeded to come out with it in print, and then of being told, when I have used it again, that I had borrowed it without acknowledgment from that student, who had indeed done just that to me! This problem acquires special complexity in the case of multiple authorship, which is particularly common in some of the sciences. It is difficult or impossible, when seeking to fix scholarly credit and blame or for that matter when evaluating a candidate for appointment or promotion, to determine what was contributed to the experiment by each of the dozen or more names carried on the masthead of the scientific paper—especially if, as often happens, the names are listed alphabetically. Professor Robert K. Merton of Columbia University, who is probably our leading sociologist of science, has cataloged dozens of instances of what he calls "doublets" and even "triplets" in the history of science, well documented instances of two or even three thinkers arriving at the same "discovery" independently of each other; the discovery of the calculus by Newton and Leibnitz is probably the best known case. That independence of discovery may, however, be seriously compromised in an atmosphere of competitiveness, where a scholarly reputation—or the next grant—can depend on being able to "scoop" other workers in the same field of investigation. It is a major teaching responsibility of universities to begin to pay closer attention to this problem of "the ethics of acknowledgments," and, once more both by example and by precept, to inculcate in each successive generation of researchers a scrupulous observance of this moral obligation and of the strict limitation that it places upon the individual's search for truth.

4. Yet is not only my debt to other scholars, past and present, that I have the obligation to acknowledge when presenting the results of my research; nor is it only the implicit initial hypothesis whose presence I must recognize when I describe how I have been brought to this conclusion. I must also describe and acknowledge the special assumptions and ideological presuppositions that I have carried into both the program of my research and my formulation of its outcome. That obligation, to be sure, is easier to state than it is to carry out, above all because of the nature of such assumptions. As a passage that I have often quoted from Alfred North Whitehead's *Science and the Modern World* (New York, 1948, pp. 49–50) puts it:

> "When you are criticizing the philosophy of an epoch, do not chiefly direct your attention to those intellectual positions which its exponents feel it necessary explicitly to defend. There will be some fundamental assumptions which adherents of all the variant systems within the epoch unconsciously presuppose. Such assumptions appear so obvious that people do not know what they are assuming because no other way of putting things has ever occurred to them. With these assumptions a certain limited number of types of philosophic systems are possible, and this group of systems constitutes the philosophy of the epoch."

But there are also many such assumptions which thinkers and scholars do not "unconsciously presuppose," but which they consciously espouse and by which they ex-

plicitly shape their conclusions. As Stephen Jay Gould
has shown, one such assumption with far-reaching consequences in the history of science during the nineteenth
and twentieth centuries was the teleology which Charles
Darwin supposed to be evident in the evolution of species,
from the less perfect to the more perfect. It was one of the
fallacies of the Enlightenment—or, at any rate, of some
thinkers in the period of the Enlightenment—to suppose
that there not only should be, but could be, a presupposi-
tionless search for truth and therefore a nonideological
statement of the results of such a search. But if that was
indeed a fallacy of the Enlightenment, our own greater
danger, I would urge, may now lie on the other side of the
question. Both the powerful critique of ideology by
Marxist analysis and the devastating exposure of hidden
assumptions by Freudian thought may, if we are not
careful, become an excuse for a relativism according to
which all formulations of truth are taken to be in fact
nothing more than veiled statements of ideological bias.
What is needed above all is a readiness to discuss such
assumptions and biases, even and including the biases of
theology and metaphysics—as well as (may I be permitted to add) the bias against theology and metaphysics,
combined as it so often is with an ignorance about both
metaphysics and theology, that characterizes many
thinkers and scholars in the modern university.

5. These general considerations of the pressing need
within the universities for greater attention to the necessary limitations that are placed upon the individual's
search for truth and of the social responsibilities which
that search implies must not, however, be construed in
such a way as to obscure the particularities, beyond such
general considerations, that can best be passed from one

generation to another within each specific field and discipline in the university. General principles are helpful, in fact indispensable; but only the experienced scholar and scientist can know the special limitations and the special temptations in the field. We probably do need to have within the university certain colleagues whose scholarly responsibility it is to think about such issues in a comprehensive and generalized context; they have traditionally been part of the department of philosophy, and there are some hopeful signs that professors of philosophy are willing—are still willing, or perhaps are willing once again—to take that responsibility upon themselves. Nevertheless, only I as a practicing historian am in a position to see, from the development of the discipline and the case studies of scholars in the field, what are all the occupational hazards to which historians are especially vulnerable. It deserves mention that the most effective identifications of these occupational hazards of the historian during our own century have come from working historians such as, to mention only a few, Herbert Butterfield, R. G. Collingwood, and Wilhelm Dilthey. It is not a minor factor to add that if one is concerned, as I am here on the basis of my assignment, "to address the topic of the university's role in developing individualism and preparing students to discharge their social responsibilities," that pedagogical role is one that the university will be able to carry out most effectively in this specific laboratory or in that specific seminar room, rather than on a public platform or pulpit. Having long urged that the history of each science and field of study ought to be part of the curriculum for the preparation of its future practitioners by introducing them to their intellectual grandparents, I would add that there seems to be no more effective method for pointing object lessons about each of these limitations on the individual's search for truth than an acquaintance with classic examples of scholars who have been committed to the search, conscious of its limitations, and successful in coping with them—or, conversely, who have fallen victim to a confusion of means and ends or to an insensitivity about the problem of hypothesis or to an ambition to claim priority. Some fields of study are much further along than others in developing the pedagogical techniques for this task; I have, for example, been quite impressed with the work that some of my colleagues in the biomedical sciences have been doing to assist both the practitioners and the students in addressing these problems.

If I had to give an entire course, rather than a single lecture, on my topic, "The Individual's Search for Truth—and Its Limitations," I think I would select, as the textbook for the course, Goethe's *Faust*, from which I earlier quoted the familiar epigram about heritage and task. For Faust is a scholar who has become weary in the individual's search for truth, who has, as he says in his opening soliloquy, "thoroughly studied, with fervent effort, philosophy, jurisprudence, and medicine—and, alas, theology, too" (lines 354-357), but without finding what he has striven so hard to achieve. He has, moreover, given up on the effort of ever being able to teach anyone anything that would "improve and convert [*bessern und bekehren*]" his fellow human beings (lines 372-373). Increasingly, therefore, he has been turning away from the search for truth and invoking the darker powers of sorcery, which ultimately leads him to fall into league with the devil, under a contract specifying that the devil may take him away when he says to any moment (lines 1699-

1702): "Bide a while, you are so beautiful!" In one of the statements of the leitmotiv of the play, the devil declares (lines 1851–1855): "If you will only despise reason and scholarship, the height of human powers, and if you will permit the spirit of lies to overpower you with works of deceit and sorcery—then I've got you for sure!" With the aid of the satanic power, the erstwhile scholar is able to amass great power and wealth, always craving still more, until finally all that stands in his way is the humble cabin of one poor couple. But it is in confrontation with that couple that Faust, practically for the first time, begins to recognize not only that the individual's search for truth does have limitations, but that it does have social responsibilities to discharge. He finally discovers that he can use his powers of mind to open up new opportunities for the lives of millions to be "active and free [*tätigfrei*]" (lines 11562–11564). What he longs for now is to "stand on a free soil with a free people" (lines 11579–11580). To this "supreme moment," a moment not any longer of self-indulgence but of moral and social responsibility, he is finally willing to say (lines 11581–11586): "Bide a while, you are so beautiful!" And therefore, instead of being dragged down to hell on the basis of his contract with the devil, he is saved—saved, as one of the choruses says, because "This man has learned, and he will teach us" (lines 12082–12083), and because his search for truth is unending and he himself will go on learning, learning indeed from Gretchen, the very person who had been the first victim of his self-indulgence (lines 12092–12093).

It is probably obvious by now that I am writing a book about Goethe's *Faust*, having first given it as a series of lectures at Southwestern University in Georgetown,

Texas, in the spring of 1993. But even this vignette should be an indication of the depth of insight available in that classic work, specifically for the issue to which this Andrew R. Cecil Lecture, and indeed the entire Andrew R. Cecil Lectureship, has been devoted.